SCIENCE AND FICTION

SCIENCE AND FICTION

BY

PATRICK MOORE F.R.A.S.

AUTHOR OF
"GUIDE TO THE MOON"
"GUIDE TO THE PLANETS"
"SUNS, MYTHS AND MEN"
ETC.

FOLCROFT LIBRARY EDITIONS 1970

Limited to 150 Copies

SCIENCE AND FICTION

BY
PATRICK MOORE F.R.A.S.

AUTHOR OF
"GUIDE TO THE MOON"
"GUIDE TO THE PLANETS"
"SUNS, MYTHS AND MEN"
ETC.

GEORGE G. HARRAP & CO. LTD
LONDON TORONTO WELLINGTON SYDNEY

First published in Great Britain 1957
by GEORGE G. HARRAP & CO. LTD
182 High Holborn, London, W.C.1

Copyright. All rights reserved

Composed in Baskerville type and printed by Elliott Bros. & Yeoman Ltd, Liverpool
Made in Great Britain

ACKNOWLEDGMENTS

Of the many who have helped in the preparation of this book, I must give my particular thanks to Arthur Sellings and to Lars Helander, both of whom have sent me books, magazines, and general information which has been of the utmost value.

I must, however, stress that the opinions put forward here are entirely my own, and that neither Mr Sellings nor Mr Helander can be held responsible for them in any way. They may well disagree with everything I have written, and this applies also to others who have given me valuable assistance: W. F. Temple, David P. Barcroft, Mary Elwyn Patchett, Werner Buedeler, and John Collings.

I must also express my thanks to my mother, who drew the "benevolent B.E.M." shown on the dust jacket.

It is hardly necessary to add that some published works, in particular J. O. Bailey's *Pilgrims through Space and Time* and Marjorie Hope Nicholson's *Voyages to the Moon*, have been invaluable for purposes of reference, though, where such authors allude to earlier books, I have done my best to avoid duplicating any of their descriptions, and have in every case consulted the original works under discussion.

1956   P.M.

273467

CONTENTS

	INTRODUCTION	page	9
1.	FROM LEGEND TO FICTION		13
2.	BIRDS, DEMONS, AND DEW		21
3.	THE GENIUS OF VERNE		43
4.	H. G. WELLS		63
5.	BUG-EYED MONSTERS—AND OTHERS		71
6.	THE MODERN MAGAZINE		86
7.	THE NEW OUTLOOK IN SCIENCE FICTION		93
8.	JUVENILE SCIENCE FICTION		104
9.	FACT OR FICTION?		108
10.	"INTERESTING, BUT IMPROBABLE . . ."		121
11.	MUTANTS AND ROBOTS		133
12.	TIME TRAVEL		139
13.	DISEMBODIED MINDS		148
14.	STORIES WITH A MESSAGE		154
15.	THE RÔLE OF THE ARTIST		160
16.	COMMENT AND REVIEW		163
17.	SOUND, STAGE, AND SCREEN		166
18.	THE FUTURE OF SCIENCE FICTION		181
	APPENDIX: A SUGGESTION REGARDING SCIENCE FICTION		186
	INDEX		190

INTRODUCTION

SCIENCE fiction has become a part of our everyday life. We read it in books, in articles, and in gaily-covered magazines; we listen to it on the wireless; we find it in strip-cartoon form, staring at us from the daily papers; we watch it on television. We cannot escape from it, even if we want to do so, and there is no choice but to accept it as a distinct branch of literature.

The mere idea of classing science fiction as 'literature' will cause many people to hold up their hands in dismay. To them, science fiction is linked with the ray-gun, the tentacled invader from Mars, and—most significant of all—the horror comic. We have to admit that horror comics and some of the modern publications are not unrelated, but science fiction is capable of breaking free from its disreputable past associations. The present book is an attempt to give a brief history of the subject, so that the position may be analysed.

It would be wrong to suggest that all science fiction descends from the horror comics and the 'pulp magazines' of the 1930's. Much of it is entirely distinct, and it is a great pity that all works with a scientific background tend to become tarred with the same brush. The position has improved during the last two or three years; but even though the pendulum is swinging, it has not yet completed half a beat.

To deal fully with all branches of science fiction would need a work the size of an encyclopædia, and it is not claimed that the present book is exhaustive. I have dealt mainly with stories which have an interplanetary background, partly because the interplanetary romance is certainly the most popular branch of scientific fiction. However, the comments I have made apply with equal force to other twigs of the tree.

Another point of vital importance concerns the question: "What is science fiction?" Do we limit ourselves to H. G. Wells, Edgar Rice Burroughs, and Dan Dare, or do we extend the field to include stories such as Olaf Stapledon's *Star Maker* and C. S. Lewis's *Out of the Silent Planet*, which are in the nature of social or philosophical studies? Do the old classics, such as Kepler's *Somnium* and Bishop Godwin's *Man in the Moone*, fit into the picture at all?

Opinion is sharply divided, and I propose, therefore, to take the wider point of view, with the full knowledge that many readers and critics will disagree. Any story with a scientific background will be considered eligible for discussion, since otherwise it would be very difficult to trace the theme through the ages and to arrive at any conclusions about present and future trends.

The general theme of my book will be clear enough. I hope to show that, while horror comics and unpleasant adult stories do linger on, and are definitely harmful, there is a type of science fiction which is good literature as well as being good entertainment. Much of this, though not all, is based upon sound science, and thus plays a useful part in the propagation of knowledge. Many people who would refuse to study a popular scientific book are only too ready to read science fiction; if they learn some genuine science in the process, so much the better. We can, in fact, separate the stories into two distinct types:

1. Those which are scientifically inaccurate.
2. Those which are as accurate as they can be made in the light of our present knowledge, though a good deal of licence must necessarily be allowed.

I read my first science-fiction story at the age of eight, when I came across a 1908 copy of *Young England*, a now defunct magazine for boys, and found there a long novel by Fenton Ash called *A Son of the Stars*. I read it avidly, and

Introduction

journeyed with the two young heroes across space to Mars, a fascinating world with a red sky, towering mountains, and two shining moons, peopled by advanced beings who had abandoned explosives as barbarous and fought their wars with electric "rambas" which caused temporary unconsciousness but no more. I took part in the war between the good king Amando and the wicked king Faronda; I held my breath when one of the heroes was carried off by one of the giant bats that lived among the Martian peaks. When Amando triumphed in the end, I triumphed with him.

The story was inaccurate in its facts, even when we remember the state of astronomical knowledge in 1908, but to me that did not matter. It enthralled me, and in so doing it increased my interest in true astronomy. I have never quite recaptured those early thrills, but when I re-read the story not long ago I enjoyed it almost as much as ever. It was vividly written, and it held the attention from beginning to end.

Stories of this kind do good, not harm, since they are pleasant reading for children, whose ideas are obviously unformed. There are plenty of similar books in circulation to-day, and the schoolmaster or the youth leader who frowns upon all science fiction, and bans it from his library, is being narrow-minded to a degree. Bloodsucking 'Venusians' and hideous mutants should be consigned to the waste-paper basket, but they are not representative. All branches of literature have undesirable relations, and science fiction is no exception.

Contrary to popular belief, science fiction is not a new development arising solely out of twentieth-century advances in upper-atmosphere research, atomic structure, and rocketry. These developments have, of course, had a great effect, which has not always been beneficial, but if we want to trace the story to its beginnings we must go back to Ancient Greece. Man has always been intrigued by the idea of travelling to other worlds, and if he cannot do so in fact he is eager to do so in imagination.

So let us forget rockets, telescopes, and space-stations for the moment, and journey backward in time. Only then shall we really be able to appreciate what science fiction is, and how it began.

1

FROM LEGEND TO FICTION

It is usually claimed that science fiction begins with the famous *True History* written by the Greek satirist, Lucian of Samosata, in the second century A.D. This is probably correct, since if any earlier space stories were written they have not come down to us. However, it may not be out of place to say something about the earlier myths and legends.

Science fiction could not begin so long as there was no true science, and the earliest men, our remote ancestors who lived among the ice-sheets of the last glacial period, can have had no real conception of the nature of the universe. To them, the Sun and Moon were gods; the Earth was flat, and the heavens revolved round it once a day. Even when the first great civilizations sprang up, science remained more or less at a standstill. Sometimes it was held that the Earth floated upon a limitless ocean, while other races believed it to be perched on the back of a huge tortoise. The idea that it might be only one among many worlds was certainly not considered at all.

One myth from Ancient China is worth re-telling, since it is typical of many others. It is related that on one occasion a herd of elephants came to drink from a sheet of water known as the Moon Lake, and in so doing trampled upon the local hare population. When they next appeared, the leader of the hares pointed out that the elephants were undoubtedly annoying the Moon-Goddess by disturbing her reflection in the water. The elephants were quick to see that this was most injudicious, and they departed hastily, leaving the hares in peace.

Many of the old legends are concerned with the "Man in the Moon," and it is easy to see why, since the outlines of the dark plains do give some impression of a human form if one's imagination is allowed full rein. Some races, however, disturbed the lunar peace by introducing a Woman as well. Hares, frogs, toads, and other creatures followed suit, until the mythological Moon ended by being a veritable zoo. Fortunately, none of the inhabitants appeared to need modern protective devices such as space-suits.

The earliest peoples divided the stars into groups or constellations, and named them after animals and common objects, but they failed to progress beyond the stage of simple star-watching. True astronomy began about 600 B.C., with the rise of Greek philosophy. The Greeks brought about a revolution in human thought, and before long they made their first important astronomical discovery: the Earth is not flat, but is shaped like a sphere.

Progress did not come all at once. Xenophanes of Colophon, who lived about 500 B.C., held that the Sun was made of "clouds set on fire," and that it was extinguished when it dipped into the sea at nightfall, so that a new Sun had to be created every morning. Philolaus, even later, thought the Sun to be a glass disk reflecting the light of the universe, while his ideas about the Moon and planets were equally strange. It was Anaxagoras of Clazomenæ, one of the greatest thinkers of Ancient Greece, who first stated that the Moon is "a solid, having in it mountains, plains and ravines." In one sentence, he opened up the way not only for astronomy, but for what we now call science fiction. If the Moon resembled the Earth, it might be inhabited; moreover, it might be reached.

The amount of work accomplished by the Greek savants was truly remarkable. No less important were their contributions to literature, and one of the later Greek writers, Plutarch, turned his attention to the heavens in general and the Moon in particular. About A.D. 70 he produced his *De Facie in Orbe Lunæ* (*Concerning the Face in the Orb of the Moon*), which was only one step removed from science fiction.

From Legend to Fiction   15

Plutarch was not primarily a scientist. His fame rests mainly on his *Parallel Lives*, a book which has been of great value to later historians, and he also wrote upward of sixty essays of varying literary quality. *De Facie in Orbe Lunæ* is long, rambling, and apparently incomplete. Part of it appears to be an attempt to sum up what was then known about the Moon, while another part is pure fantasy, even though it may not have been intended to be taken as such.

Plutarch's scientific speculations do not concern us at the moment, but his fantasies do. Though he agreed with Anaxagoras that the Moon is a second Earth, with mountains, valleys, and ravines scattered across its surface, he rejected the idea of human inhabitants, and replaced them with demons. The second part of his essay is in dialogue form, and describes the wanderings of departed souls as they glided between Earth and Moon.

Some of Plutarch's ideas were very strange. It was said, for instance, that the lunar demons could leave the Moon when they chose, and could descend to Earth, where they spoke to living men through the mouths of Oracles such as that of Delphi. Souls who were undeveloped or violent were not permitted to remain on the Moon, but were sent firmly back to Earth until they had learned the error of their ways. This theme was followed later on by many writers, including the famous Bishop Godwin, but the original idea is due to Plutarch.

It is not clear how seriously Plutarch took his own speculations, but only half a century later came the first real science-fiction story. This was, of course, Lucian's *True History*, and is well worth close study, partly because of its ingenuity and partly because of its literary value.

Lucian was one of the most brilliant satirists of the ancient world. He combined a cool brain with a gift for fluent, easy writing, and he also possessed a strong sense of humour. He even tells us something about himself. Apparently he spent a good deal of his school time in scraping the wax off his tablets and making models of animals and men, so that he was apprenticed to his uncle with a view to his becoming a sculptor. He made a bad beginning by dropping a marble slab, shattering it into several pieces, and was so soundly thrashed for it that he ran away and returned home. But though unsuccessful as a sculptor, he became eminently successful as a writer. He produced a great many works, and one of those best remembered to-day is his interplanetary story. This is not only because of the recent growth of interest in all things celestial; it was first translated into English as long ago as 1634, and has always been regarded as one of the best and most amusing of his works.

The very name sums it up. In his own words, the story describes things which he had "neither seen nor suffered nor learned from another, things which are not and never could have been; therefore my readers should by no means believe them." In other words, the *True History* is made up of lies from beginning to end—but they are lies exceedingly well told.

Positive knowledge of the world was then confined mainly to the Mediterranean zone, and Lucian sensibly went farther afield, to the wild and unknown region west of what we now call the Straits of Gibraltar, known to the ancients as the Pillars of Hercules. The first part of the *True History* is comparatively conventional, and deals with the adventures of a party of sailors sailing through the Pillars across the ocean beyond. After eighty days' rough sailing they came to an island on which they found a Greek inscription: "This was the limit of the voyage of Heracles and Dionysus." Dionysus, the wine-god, had been thoughtful enough to leave an excellent supply of liquor on the island, and it was at once decided to make a short stay there before proceeding further. After sailing away once more—not without regrets, one imagines—their ship was caught up in a whirlwind, and they found themselves being carried upward on the crest of a tremendous waterspout. "Upon a sudden," says Lucian, "a whirlwind caught us, which turned our ship round about, and lifted us up three thousand furlongs into the air." For

From Legend to Fiction

seven days and seven nights they flew on, with the ocean far out of sight below them, until at last they saw what they took to be land: "a great country in the air, like a shining island." They were within a few miles of the hitherto unattainable Moon.

Their appearance caused something of a stir. Almost at once they saw some warriors mounted upon "horse vultures," tremendous three-headed birds, and the hapless sailors were arrested and brought as prisoners before the King of the Moon. They were astounded to find that this king was Endymion, who had evidently decided that it was time to wake up. They next learned that they had arrived at a momentous time, since Endymion was engaged in a war against the ruler of the Sun, King Phæthon. Each claimed the right to colonize "Lucifer"—Venus, the Evening Star—and each had mustered an impressive army. Endymion's forces included sixty million men, eighty thousand horse-vulture troops, and twenty thousand soldiers who rode birds which were of enormous size and were covered with a dense shield of vegetation sufficient to conceal the riders. Nor was this all. There were also spiders, each larger than an island, and thirty thousand flea-riders. Phæthon was not to be outdone; his force included an army of ants.

Lucian also gave a detailed description of the Moon-Men themselves. They were naturally far more advanced than the people of Earth, and anything unclean or impure was abhorrent to them. Sex was either unknown or ignored, and even when a Moon-Man died he merely dissolved into smoke, so that no remains should be left for burial. Small wonder that the sailors hastened to enlist in Endymion's army. They took part in battle, and it is said that the slaughter was so great that the heavens were stained red with blood.

The adventurers returned eventually to Earth, landing their ship safely in the ocean, but were promptly swallowed by an immense sea-serpent over a hundred miles long. They met with many dangers inside the creature's belly, and at last managed to sail out between the monster's teeth, to find themselves at the "Fortunate Islands" in company with the souls of the heroes and philosophers of antiquity. Lucian was too clever a writer to allow himself to end his tale on a note of anticlimax, and the story finishes rather suddenly, with a promise that the rest will be told in later books.

This is science fiction pure and simple. Lucian's seamen are the logical ancestors of the rocketeers and space-cadets of to-day, and his plot has been imitated time and time again. We have the initial voyage, the discovery of advanced beings on another world, the battle in space—how many times have we not read much the same thing in books, in magazines, and in strip cartoons? It is noteworthy, too, that Lucian was not in the least concerned with scientific accuracy. His aim was to ridicule some older writers who had written tales almost as extravagant, but had tried to pass them off as being true.

Yet—and this is an important point—the *True History* is pleasant reading from end to end. Nor is there any suggestion of a menace to Earth, a theme which has obsessed many more modern writers and has given their works a depressing sameness. Lucian may have been a satirist, but he was a good-natured one, and only when attacking humbug and insincerity did he become in the least biting.

Though the *True History* stands by itself, Lucian did produce one more interplanetary story, *Icaromenippus*. The main difference between the two is that while the sailors of the first book had no idea of reaching the Moon, and were hurled upward quite by chance, Icaromenippus set out with that object in mind. "I saw the stars scattered carelessly up and down the heaven," he says, "and I much desired to learn what matter the Sun was made of; but the greatest cause of marvel to me was the Moon." He therefore determined to make a pair of wings so that he could fly up and investigate for himself.

Instead of constructing artificial wings, he took one from a vulture and the other from an eagle. One might imagine that the result would have been somewhat lop-sided, but the tiresome theory of flight had not then been developed, and

From Legend to Fiction

Icaromenippus was therefore able to learn how to soar without much difficulty. At last he was ready, and he took off from the summit of Mount Olympus. We are told how he turned slowly with the Moon, and how he saw the Earth beneath him; how he succeeded in his quest, and landed safely upon the Moon itself; and how he "struck up directly towards Heaven," leaving the Sun far behind him, and flying at will among the stars. Unfortunately the divine beings of Olympus resented the intrusion of a mere mortal, and the messenger of the gods, Hermes, was dispatched to escort him back home. After his return to his native planet, Icaromenippus' wings were confiscated in order to prevent his making a second attempt.

Here, again, Lucian has had his imitators in plenty. The idea of divine displeasure at the invasion of space has persisted all through the ages. As recently as August 1955 the announcement of the American space-satellite programme was denounced by one earnest cleric as wicked and irreligious, while the theme has been used *ad nauseam* in stories of all kinds. Yet although Lucian's Olympians were displeased, they were not revengeful. Icaromenippus was not scorched by a death-ray, blasted by an atomic cannon, or deprived of his reason; he was merely taken gently but firmly back to where he belonged.

So much, then, for Lucian. If he could have read some of the later works to be written upon the same theme he would have been vastly amused, but in classical times he stood alone, while his two interplanetary stories were not emulated for fifteen hundred years. One reason for this was, no doubt, that with the end of Greek greatness literature came virtually to a standstill. The Dark Ages descended upon Europe. The Roman Empire, which had at least maintained law and order of a kind, fell to pieces, and the hordes of the barbarians were concerned with fighting and plunder rather than with the arts. When the revival did come it was slow.

Science was similarly halted. The Greeks had played their

part, but when they fell into obscurity there was no one to follow them. It was only with the gradual emergence of Europe in its modern form that progress was resumed, and it was a long time indeed before the minds of men turned back towards the stars.

2

BIRDS, DEMONS, AND DEW

It was fitting that the next great science-fiction story should be written by a man who was not a mere teller of tales, but one of the most brilliant mathematical astronomers of all time. He was Johann Kepler, who first drew up the celebrated "laws of planetary motion" that bear his name, and who proved once and for all that the Earth revolves round the Sun.

As a matter of fact, there is some doubt as to whether Kepler's *Somnium* was completed before another famous but totally different work, Godwin's *Man in the Moone*. We do not know the exact date of either, and so the question must remain unanswered, but it is of no particular importance. The *Somnium* was certainly the first to be published, since it appeared in 1634, while the *Man in the Moone* followed four years later. Moreover, Kepler's work is basically the more interesting of the two, though from a purely literary point of view it is inferior to Godwin's.

Kepler himself had a curious and rather unhappy life, and we can see the influence of this all the way through his *Somnium*. He was born at Weil, in Württemberg, in 1571. His father was well-connected, but was an idle, shiftless adventurer who finally deserted his family and left them to fend for themselves. Johann was scarcely more fortunate in his other parent, since his mother was an ignorant woman with a vitriolic tongue and a temper that was, to say the least of it, abominable. To make matters worse, the boy caught smallpox when only four years old, and even when the disease left him he was never free from its after-effects. All through his life he suffered from ill-health, and his eyesight was weak.

Luckily he was of a scientific turn of mind, and by 1594 he had advanced sufficiently to obtain for himself the post of Professor of Astronomy in the University of Gratz. Professors of astronomy have always been misunderstood creatures. They are popularly supposed to be wizened, gnarled old men with long white beards, who perch themselves in observatories on the tops of inaccessible mountains and spend their time 'watching the stars,' whatever that singularly futile phrase can be construed to mean. Actually, the modern professional astronomer does very little star-watching. He is concerned mainly with photographing remote galaxies, and more time is spent in the laboratory than in the observatory dome. In Kepler's day, however, the duties of a professor were concerned largely with the fossil 'science' of astrology.

Most people know something about astrology, and it is sometimes quite entertaining to pore over the birthday forecasts in the less serious-minded Sunday papers to see what Fate and the Government have in store for us, but from a scientific viewpoint astrology is pure nonsense. Opinions in the sixteenth century were different, and Kepler himself was a convinced astrologer, so that he fitted excellently into his new position at Gratz.

Not long after his appointment he published his first book, a volume with the engaging title of *Prodromus Dissertationum Cosmographicarum Seu Mysterium Cosmographicum*. It is not light reading, and it contains a very few grains of truth mixed up with a great deal of astrology and mysticism, so that its scientific value is practically nil. However, it had far-reaching effects. Tycho Brahe, the colourful and eccentric Danish astronomer, was looking for an assistant; Kepler's book appealed to him, and in 1600 Kepler joined Tycho in Prague, where the Dane was living.

Tycho's life-story would require a book to itself. It had started off on a high note of melodrama, when as a baby he had been unceremoniously kidnapped by his uncle. Later he

Birds, Demons, and Dew

was involved in an amazing number of disputes and quarrels, one of which resulted in his having part of his nose sliced off in a duel. Having repaired the damage by means of gold, silver, and wax, he built an observatory on the Baltic islet of Hven, and laboured there for twenty years, making very accurate observations of the positions of the stars and planets. It is safe to say that no scientific institution like Tycho's has ever been found before or since. The staff included a monkey and a pet dwarf, and there was even a prison, since Tycho was landlord of all Hven and ruled it in the manner of a particularly ferocious feudal baron. Finally he was driven out, and left his native country for good. Fortunately for him the Holy Roman Emperor, Rudolph II, held him in great respect, and provided him with funds sufficient to keep him in comfort for the rest of his life.

The battle between the old idea of an Earth-centred universe and the alternative conception of a central Sun had been raging ever since 1546. It was natural enough for the ancient philosophers to suppose that the Earth lay at rest in the middle of the universe, but even by the end of Greek times some disquieting facts had come to light, since the planets were not behaving as they should. Their movements against the starry background had been studied closely and with remarkable accuracy, and it was clear that the theory of circular movement around a stationary Earth was inadequate. This was recognized by the last of the astronomers of the Greek school, Ptolemy, and he accordingly described a system by which each planet revolved round the Earth in a small circle, or "epicycle," the centre of which itself revolved round the Earth in a perfect circle.

This Ptolemaic system, as it is called (despite the fact that Ptolemy himself was not responsible for it), was accepted for over a thousand years, mainly because any criticism of it was regarded as impious. The first serious challenge, that of 1546, came from a Polish canon named Copernicus. Copernicus knew quite well that Ptolemy's arrangement was inaccurate, even when all the various epicycles had been allowed for, and he therefore dethroned the Earth from its central position and put the Sun there instead.

Such an alteration improved matters, but there were still difficulties. Like Ptolemy, Copernicus thought that the paths of the planets must be circular—since the circle is the "perfect" form, and nothing short of perfection could be allowed in the heavens. Discrepancies still arose, and Tycho Brahe never accepted the Copernican theory. Instead he drew up a scheme of his own, based upon that favoured by the ancient Egyptians, according to which the planets circled the Sun, but the Sun itself circled the Earth.

When Tycho died in 1601, he left his entire store of accurate observations to Kepler. Kepler used them well. He concentrated particularly upon the movements of Mars, and found that the observed wanderings could be explained neither by circular motion round the Sun nor by circular motion round the Earth. After years of work he found the answer. The planets revolve round the Sun indeed, but they do so not in circles, but in ellipses. Eventually he worked out his three famous Laws of Planetary Motion, and in the first of them he stated that "the planets revolve round the Sun in ellipses, the Sun lying at one of the foci of the ellipse, while the other focus is empty."

This tremendous work could not be done in a hurry, and, in fact, it took Kepler many years. The first two Laws were not satisfactorily worked out until 1609, eight years after Tycho's death; the third Law was published after a further lapse of ten years as part of a book called *De Harmonice Mundi*, which contained some brilliant mathematical science coupled with the usual mysticism. One of Kepler's loves was the old idea of the Music of the Spheres. The various planets were thought to emit wonderful music, inaudible to human ears, and performed for the sole benefit of one supreme being whose soul resided in the Sun. So far as is known, nobody suggested that the erratic movements of comets might be due to celestial jazz.

Kepler was always troubled by illness and poverty, but

Birds, Demons, and Dew

further complications arose in 1620, when his seventy-four-year-old mother was arrested on the charge of being a witch. Catherine Kepler must indeed have looked and acted rather like the conventional witch of the fairy-tale, and her acid tongue had earned her enemies in plenty, so that her arrest was not particularly surprising. Sir Rupert Murgatroyd's methods of dealing with witches were commonplace at that time, and though Johann must have realized his mother's shortcomings, he had no desire to see her burned at the stake. He rushed back to Württemberg, and spent a complete year working for her release. Catherine was brought to trial, but after being kept in prison for thirteen months she was acquitted; she died shortly afterwards.

All these events are important in connexion with Kepler's venture into the realm of science fiction. We can see the sort of man he was; his was a dual personality, part of his nature coldly scientific and the other part frankly mystical. He might have been expected to combine both aspects in any work of fiction, and this is precisely what he did. Discounting Plutarch's essay, which can hardly be regarded as fiction, Kepler's story was the first in which the Moon was described as it was genuinely believed to be, but on the other hand the space-flight itself involved the supernatural.

Modern authors ranging from Edgar Rice Burroughs to C. S. Lewis have adopted similar methods; but whereas a twentieth-century supernatural voyage can be criticized as being a cowardly evasion, Kepler can hardly be blamed for using demon power. Rockets and space-guns were yet to come, but Kepler certainly believed in demons, so that there seemed no reason why they should not be put to work.

The hero of the *Somnium* is a young Icelander, Duracotus, whose parents were fisher-folk. Duracotus had no clear recollection of his father, who had died at the advanced age of 150 while the boy was still young, but his mother, Fiolxhilda, was very much to be reckoned with. Fiolxhilda was a "wise woman," who earned her living by providing sailors with bags of magical herbs. One day Duracotus tampered with one of the bags, and destroyed it. His mother was so angry that she handed him over to the sailor who had been promised the charm, and when the ship left Iceland Duracotus left with it as an unwilling member of the crew.

The ship sailed across the Atlantic, until at last it reached the coast of Denmark. Duracotus had been of little help as a seaman, and the captain had no further use for him, so he decided to use him solely as a messenger-boy. In Denmark lived the famous astronomer Tycho Brahe, and Duracotus was dispatched to take Tycho some letters which the captain wished to be delivered.

Tycho received the boy kindly, and saw that he was a youth of real talent. He even offered to instruct him in the wonders of astronomy, and Duracotus was only too ready to learn; he spent five years on Hven, and when at last he left for home he knew almost as much about the heavens as Tycho himself. Yet in spite of everything he could not forget his mother, and when he arrived back in Iceland he was overjoyed to find her alive and well.

Duracotus soon found that there was little he could teach Fiolxhilda about astronomy. He himself had been instructed by a great scientist, but Tycho, brilliant though he was, was a man and nothing more. Fiolxhilda's teacher was a demon, who lived not in Scandinavia, but in "Levania," the Moon.

Fiolxhilda was cautious, but at last she made up her mind to reveal some of her secrets. Both Levania and "Volva," the Earth, contain demons; but in the ordinary way no demons can cross from one world to the other, because they hate light, and the rays of the Sun are too brilliant. Occasionally, however, the shadow of the Earth falls on to the Moon, and for an hour or two there is a bridge of darkness across which the demons can pass at will.

The Moon is not self-luminous, and shines only because it reflects the light of the Sun. Like any other solid and non-radiating body, the Earth casts a shadow in space, so that when the Sun, Earth, and Moon move into a straight line, with the Earth in the middle, this shadow cuts the sunlight

Birds, Demons, and Dew

off from the Moon's surface. This is what is known as a lunar eclipse, and if the Moon passes wholly into the shadow the eclipse is said to be total. Generally the Moon does not vanish completely, since the Earth's blanket of air bends some of the sun-rays on to the lunar disk, but instead of shining with its normal brilliance, the Moon turns a dim, sometimes coppery colour. Eclipses do not happen every month, owing to the tilt of the Moon's orbit, but on an average there are at least three per year.

Duracotus wanted to make the journey for himself. This could be managed, since the demons were obliging enough to take human tourists now and then, and at last all was ready. By means of her charms Fiolxhilda summoned the demons of Levania, and then "withdrawing from me into the nearest cross-roads," as Duracotus wrote, "then returned; and commanding silence with the palm of her right hand outstretched, sat down near me. Scarcely had we covered our heads with a cloth, as is the custom, then behold, there came the sound of a voice . . ."

So far the story of the *Somnium* has been pure fantasy, but from now on we start to find a mixture of true sixteenth-century science. It is stressed that the journey along the bridge of shadow must always be far from comfortable, as human beings are affected by coldness and by the lack of air. This latter point is significant, and here at least Kepler's story is more plausible than Lucian's.

The old philosophers had thought the air to extend to the farthest reaches of the universe, but Kepler knew better. Centuries before, the Arab astronomers had calculated that the atmosphere can extend upward for not more than a thousand miles. This was a remarkably good guess; nowadays it is known that air resistance becomes very slight above only 120 miles or so, while studies of the electrical phenomena known as auroræ polaris, or Polar Lights, have shown that even at altitudes of 700 and 800 miles there is a trace of air left. On the other hand, it is a quarter of a million miles to the Moon, and Kepler reasoned that most of the journey must be done in vacuum. Duracotus was accordingly given an anæsthetic, or "dozing draught," to ease the discomfort; he was also given sponges, which were moistened and held to the nostrils. Short of equipping his hero with a space-suit, Kepler could hardly have done any better, and this is the first indication that the *Somnium* is meant to be something rather more than a mere story.

Even more significant is the fact that Kepler did not overlook the effect of what we now call gravity. He had discovered how the planets move; he had not discovered why they move in such a way, but he was certainly on the right track. He describes how the demons' part was done when they had pulled Duracotus up to the point where the Moon's force balances that of the Earth. After this point had been reached they simply let go, and allowed their passenger to fall towards the Moon on his own. We have, in fact, the first indication of the "neutral point" between the two bodies, later to be used—or, rather, misused—by no less a writer than Jules Verne.

Moreover, Duracotus relates that as soon as he arrived at the neutral point his limbs curled up like those of a spider. "When the attractions of the Moon and of the Earth equalize each other, it is as though neither of them exerted any attraction. Then the body itself, being the whole, attracts its minor parts, its limbs, because the body is the whole." Nothing could be clearer. Kepler is describing gravity. He did not understand it, of course, and even refers to it as "magnetic influence," but he is describing it none the less.

So much for the voyage itself. Kepler had to use supernatural means simply because he knew of no other, but as soon as Duracotus reaches the Moon the story becomes purely scientific. At that time it was still believed that the Moon was a smaller edition of the Earth, with air, oceans, and inhabitants. It was only a few years since Galileo had turned his first crude telescope to the heavens and had constructed the first lunar map, so Kepler had no means of guessing that the real Moon is airless, waterless, and lifeless.

Birds, Demons, and Dew

His description of our satellite is in accord with the facts as he knew them.

From the astronomer's point of view, the Moon behaves in an infuriating way inasmuch as it keeps one hemisphere turned permanently away from the Earth. It revolves round us[1] in $27\frac{1}{3}$ days, but it also spins on its axis in $27\frac{1}{3}$ days, so that there is a part of the Moon which we can never see. (The best way to show what is meant is to walk round a chair, keeping your face towards the chair-seat all the time. By the time you have completed one revolution you will have turned once on your axis; the back of your head, representing the back of the Moon, will not have been turned towards the chair at all.) This means that to an observer standing on the lunar surface the Earth will appear to remain almost stationary in the sky, while from the averted hemisphere the Earth can never be seen.

Kepler knew this, and Duracotus relates how Levania is divided into two zones, Subvolva and Privolva. From Subvolva the "Volva," or Earth, is always visible; from Privolva, never. In general, he finds that Levania is a world of extremes, with violent changes of climate, towering mountains, and deep valleys.

> The hollows of the Moon first seen by Galileo are portions below the general level, like our oceans, but their appearance makes me judge that they are swampy for the greater part. It is there that the Endymionides find the sites for the fortified cities which protect them against the swampiness as well as against the heat of the Sun, possibly also against their enemies.

Lucian's King of the Moon had been Endymion; now we find Kepler referring to the lunar inhabitants as Endymionides, but there the resemblance ends. The Moon-folk of the *Somnium* are not human either in mind or in body. Some are of a serpent-like form, while others have fins to propel them through the water, and still others crawl along

---

[1] More accurately, the Earth and the Moon revolve round their common centre of gravity. As this centre of gravity lies within the terrestrial globe, the difference is not, however, important to anybody but a mathematician.

the ground. Most are covered with fur. When a Moon creature is unwise enough to allow itself to be caught in the open near midday its outer fur is singed by the intense heat, so that the creature drops as though dead. At nightfall it revives, and the singed parts of its fur simply fall away.

Government and civilization in the terrestrial sense cannot exist on Levania, mainly because of the brief life-span of its inhabitants. In Subvolva, particularly, the creatures and plants are of monstrous size, but live for only a few lunar days. This is more or less what would be expected upon a moist, fiercely hot world, as Kepler believed the daytime Subvolva to be.

There is some truth in Duracotus' word-picture. As the Moon rotates so slowly, a 'day' there is as long as a fortnight on Earth, and the equatorial temperature can attain +216 degrees Fahrenheit, above that of boiling water. At midnight, however, this temperature drops to —250 degrees Fahrenheit, so that air would freeze. Moreover, the lunar peaks are higher than ours, both relatively and absolutely; recent measures of the lunar Leibnitz Mountains show that they attain a height of 30,000 feet, which is greater than that of Everest. The depths of the cracks or clefts are still rather uncertain, but must be considerable, so that the Moon is indeed a world of extremes. What Kepler did not know, and could not know, is that it is virtually airless and completely without liquid, so that his plants and Endymionides cannot exist outside the pages of a book.

Yet Kepler cheats us in the end. At the very beginning of his tale he tells how he himself lay down one night after a period of watching the skies, and drifted presently into a doze. At the very last we learn that the whole story has been a dream; that Duracotus, Fiolxhilda, Endymionides, and the Levanian demons were part of it, and that he awoke to find "his head covered with a cushion, and his body tangled in a rug." We see now why Kepler called his book the *Somnium*.

The main difference between the stories of Lucian and

Kepler is that the Greek satirist was writing in light-hearted vein, and was not in the least concerned whether his tale was factually correct or not, while Kepler could not break away from science. The *Somnium* is of distinct value. More clearly than in any other of his works, it shows that Kepler had a good idea of Newtonian gravitation, even though he could not put it into mathematical form. It shows, too, that he knew that the Earth's atmosphere cannot extend all the way to the Moon.

The *Somnium* is not always pleasant reading. Fiolxhilda is, of course, Catherine Kepler, while Duracotus is Johann himself, and it is rather a relief to turn away from demons and the witch-woman to a far more amusing story—the *Man in the Moone* of Godwin.

Francis Godwin, son of the Bishop of Bath and Wells, was born in 1562 and died in 1633. He studied at Christ Church, Oxford, and became first Rector of Sampford-Dorcas, in Somerset, and then Vicar of Weston-in-Zoyland. In 1587 he was appointed sub-dean of Exeter. In 1601 he published a vast catalogue of "Bishops of England since the first planting of the Christian Religion in this Island," and Elizabeth I made him Bishop of Llandaff. Later, in the reign of James I, Godwin became Bishop of Hereford. He was no doubt a worthy and sincere man, and was the author of several theological works as well as his Catalogue, but he would hardly be remembered now but for his venture into science fiction. He did not have Kepler's profound astronomical knowledge, and he never accepted the Copernican theory of the revolution of the Earth round the Sun; but he was an intelligent and highly educated man, and from a literary point of view his *Man in the Moone* far outranks the *Somnium*.

Actually Godwin was dead by the time that the *Somnium* appeared, but it seems certain that he had read a manuscript copy of it. The *Man in the Moone* was published posthumously in 1638, and we do not know quite when it was written, though some authorities believe that it was completed only a month or two before Godwin died.

At any rate, it proved extremely popular. Both the *Somnium* and Lucian's *True History*, which had been translated into English and published in 1634, had been widely read, but the *Man in the Moone* really caught hold of public imagination. It ran to six impressions during the half-century following its original appearance, and even to-day it makes amusing reading.

The central figure of the story is Domingo Gonzales, a young Spaniard of noble but impoverished family. The first part of the book is more or less conventional, and relates how Gonzales ran away from university, killed a man in a duel, and fled from Europe to the West Indies, meeting with incredible adventures on the way. The interplanetary part of the tale begins on the remote island of St Helena. St Helena is well-known to every modern schoolboy as the place where Napoleon Bonaparte spent his last years, but in Godwin's time it was just another obscure islet without permanent inhabitants, so that any number of wondrous things might well happen to a sailor who chanced to be marooned there.

Gonzales had been "grievously sick"[1] during the voyage from the West Indies, and had been landed on St Helena with no companion apart from his faithful servant, a Negro named Diego. He was far from dissatisfied. The island suited him very well; "the only paradise, I think, that the Earth yieldeth," he writes of it. He and Diego spent a pleasant year there, living on the varied and nourishing fruits that grew in plenty. There was also animal life, and birds were numerous. Particularly interesting to Gonzales were some "gansas," or wild swans, that appeared to visit the island during certain seasons of the year. They vanished in winter, so that they hibernated elsewhere, but this seemed of no great significance to the young Spaniard at the time.

For some reason or other, perhaps because he was bored,

---

[1] Except in actual titles, I have adopted the method of modernizing the spelling when quoting these old books. This policy is open to severe criticism, but it certainly makes for easier reading.

Gonzales made up his mind to tame some of these gansas. He selected thirty or forty youngsters, and soon found that they were surprisingly tractable. He taught them to fly to him at a given signal, to tow small burdens through the air, and to carry materials from him to Diego. These last experiments put a new and more daring idea into his mind. If the gansas could be trusted to tow food, why should they not tow a man on a raft?

Gonzales was cautious at first. The training of the gansas took some time, and when the aerial raft was constructed he would not trust himself in it. Instead he used a lamb, so that the first creature to fly by semi-artificial means was not a human being, but an animal. This proved to be an accurate prophecy. When the balloon was invented, a century and a half later, the first creatures to take to the skies in a clumsy hot-air 'Montgolfière' were a sheep, a cock, and a duck; and though the sheep was careless enough to kick the duck at the trying moment of take-off, all three landed safely. More recently the rocket has come into its own, and mice and monkeys have had the honour of being the first high-altitude flyers. Whether or not they appreciate the distinction must remain open to doubt.

The successful results of his first experiments made up Gonzales' mind for him, and he determined to make a trial flight himself. Accordingly he hauled his raft up to the top of a rocky cliff overlooking a river, so that if he did chance to fall he would land in the water. Then, in his own words:

> I caused Diego to advance his signal, whereupon my birds presently arose, 25 in number, and carried me over lustily to the other rock on the far side, being about a quarter of a league.... O how did my heart even swell with joy and admiration!... How often did I wish myself in the midst of Spain, that speedily I might fill the world with the fame of my glory and renown!

Unfortunately Spain was a long way away, and Gonzales was compelled to wait for a transport-ship to rescue him.

Three months later three vessels of the Indian fleet arrived, and Diego and Gonzales went aboard them, leaving their "paradise island" to its usual solitude. Gonzales was forced to take the captain into his confidence, mainly because there might otherwise have been violent objections to his bringing over twenty birds with him, but also because some members of the crew were thinking wistfully about swan pie. For a time, all went well.

Then came a crisis. The ships were attacked by the English fleet, and it became clear that Gonzales' vessel was bound to be captured or destroyed. There was only one way to escape:

> I then betook me to my gansas, put them upon my engine, and myself upon it, trusting (as indeed it happily fell out) that when the ship should split, my birds, although they wanted their signal, of themselves, and for the safeguard of their own lives . . . would make towards the land.

Even then his troubles were far from over, since the inhabitants of the new island proved decidedly hostile. Gonzales took to the air again, but this time the gansas showed no inclination to come down. Instead of alighting on the mountain-top that Gonzales had selected, they kept on ascending—higher, higher, ever higher. Then, suddenly, Gonzales found that the birds no longer had to pull strongly in order to tow him along. They had reached so great an altitude that the conditions of gravity were altered, and it was then that the truth struck him. The gansas hibernated on the Moon, and were taking him with them, whether he wanted to come or no.

Gonzales did not appear to be unduly perturbed. Unlike Duracotus in the *Somnium*, he was not provided with anything in the way of an anæsthetic, but he found that the absence of gravity made it unnecessary for him to eat or drink; indeed, his vigour of body and mind seemed to be even more pronounced than usual. Nor did he experience any difficulty in breathing. Godwin's voyage is therefore pure fantasy, but he did at least make it last for twelve days,

Birds, Demons, and Dew

whereas Duracotus is said to have passed across the bridge of shadow in only an hour or so.

At their estimated speed of 175 m.p.h., the gansas covered 50,000 miles in twelve days. Clearly there is some mistake here, as the real distance of the Moon is more than four times greater than this, so that Godwin's astronomy was at fault. It seems that he had drawn his information from Kepler's books, and had made a slip either in calculating or (more probably) in copying.

The journey was placid enough, and Gonzales went on "without interruption for eleven or twelve days, during all which time I was carried directly towards the globe or body of the Moon." At last he approached his goal, and found that "it was covered for the most part with a huge and mighty sea, those parts only being dry land which show unto us here somewhat darker than the rest of her body." He realized, too, that the Moon is not self-luminous, and shines only by reflected sunlight. Moreover, he detected small islands in the sea, so small that from Earth they were invisible to normal eyes. It is possible that Godwin was making an indirect allusion to some of the craters which are to be met with on the grey lunar plains, and which can be detected with a telescope no more powerful than that originally used by Galileo.

The mild attempts at science met with earlier in Godwin's story are abandoned as soon as Gonzales sets foot on the top of the lunar Mount Pisgah, and the tale becomes a delightful fantasy. The Moon is a true Utopia, peopled by beings who are human in form but are far in advance of Earthmen, who abhor uncleanliness as violently as Lucian's Moon-Men had done, and who speak in a language so musical that it can be written down only in note form.

Though the Moon is smaller than the Earth, Gonzales finds that its inhabitants are larger. The most important personages are some thirty feet tall, and are able to remain in the open even when the dazzling Sun and the almost equally resplendent Earth are shining together. Moon-Men of smaller stature, a mere ten to twelve feet tall, can "endure the daylight when the Earth shineth but little, but cannot endure the beams of both Earth and Sun." Gonzales himself, only six feet in height, finds that he is much the same size as the inferior lunar race of "bastard-men," who "seldom live above an age of a thousand months, which is answerable to 80 of our years; and [the superior Moon-Men] account them base creatures, even but a degree before brute beasts, employing them accordingly in all the basest and most servile offices."

Fortunately Gonzales is regarded as a distinguished visitor, and he meets with nothing but kindness from the mighty Prince Irdonzur and other members of the ruling race. For two years he remains on the Moon, and throughout his stay he is free to come and go as he pleases.

One or two points in his long description of the lunar world are worth noting. First, he finds that there is colour everywhere;

> neither black, nor white, nor yellow nor red, green nor blue, nor any colour composed of them. But if you ask me what it was; then I must tell you, it was a colour never seen in our earthly world, and therefore neither to be described unto us by any, nor to be conceived of one that never saw it. . . . Only this I can say of it, that it was the most glorious and delightful that can possibly be imagined.

Actually, colour on the real Moon is virtually lacking. The entire surface is grey, either because it is made up of grey rock or (more probably) because it is overlaid with a thin layer of ash, mainly volcanic, but with an added amount due to meteoric dust. Reds, greens, and yellows have been described now and then, but are so elusive that their existence must be regarded as dubious. I have made extensive lunar observations for the past twenty years, using telescopes ranging from small portable instruments up to some of the largest in the world, and I have yet to see any decided colour. Even Galileo and the other early observers must have known that the Moon is a world of drabness. Godwin's

Birds, Demons, and Dew 37

description may be an indication that he knew this, and was trying to paint his picture in colours which could not be seen by mortal men until they reached the lunar world.

Secondly, Godwin seems to have borrowed the old idea that since the Moon is the abode of pure and advanced beings, any Selenites who fall short of the high standard required can well be exiled to Earth, where there is already so much depravity that a little more cannot possibly matter. The Moon-Men are able to tell at once whether a newly born child is likely to prove satisfactory or not. If it shows any signs of latent wickedness it is dispatched without further delay: "the ordinary vent for them is a certain high hill in the North of America, whose people I can easily believe to be wholly descended of them." Evidently Godwin had a low opinion of the people of the New World.

Gonzales' eventual return is more or less forced upon him. Three of his gansas have already died because they have been unable to follow their normal habit of returning periodically to Earth, and the rest have begun to droop, so that further delay will mean insufficient bird-power to complete the journey. When Gonzales' final preparations are complete he bids farewell to the genial Prince Irdonzur, mounts his raft, and "lets loose the reins unto my birds, who with great greediness taking wing quickly carry me out of sight."

Whereas the outward trip to the Moon had taken twelve days, the return to Earth takes only nine. This, Gonzales explains, is due to the greater attractive power of the Earth, and at one point he finds that he is falling so quickly that disaster is imminent. Fortunately Prince Irdonzur has given him a magic jewel, which halts his threatened nose-dive and lands him safe and sound in a country which subsequently turns out to be China. The story is not over; Gonzales meets with further remarkable adventures in the Far East, which was a great deal more mysterious then than it is now, but since these adventures are not interplanetary they hardly concern us at the moment.

Godwin's whole book shows that he possessed not only a

lively imagination, but also a sense of humour, since it is obvious that the *Man in the Moone* is not meant to be taken seriously. In its day it was regarded as a classic, and many lesser writers either copied it or adapted it. In 1706, indeed, Thomas d'Urfey even wrote a play round the original plot. Certainly it became far more popular than Kepler's *Somnium*.

From a literary viewpoint the *Man in the Moone* is valuable, and from the scientific standpoint also it is worth consideration, even though most of its science was taken directly from Kepler. It certainly helped to revive the idea of a lunar voyage, which had been dead for over a thousand years. Many interplanetary stories of the next two centuries drew from it, and, ironically, it is far better remembered than the encyclopædic catalogue of English bishops, of which Godwin himself must have been far prouder.[1]

Shortly after Godwin's tale was published there appeared a work by John Wilkins entitled *The Discovery of a World in the Moone; or, a Discourse tending to prove that 'tis probable there be another Habitable World in that Planet*. Wilkins, the first Secretary of the Royal Society, was one of the earliest writers of what is now known as popular science, and he was no author of fiction, but in the second edition of his *Discovery* he added the following note: "I chanced upon a late fancy ... written by a reverend and learned bishop, in which there is delivered a very pleasant and well-contrived fancy concerning a voyage to this other world." He then outlined the plot, and added that in his view there was nothing impossible in the idea of training birds to tow a raft to the Moon, despite the obvious difficulties. It is clear that Wilkins, despite his scientific training, did not appreciate that no bird can fly in airless space, or that there are many thousands of miles of void between us and the tantalizing lunar globe.

The English publication of Lucian's *True History*, together with the works of Kepler and Godwin, aroused new interest

---

[1] The clown longs to play Hamlet; the jazz pianist dreams of symphonies. Who does not know Sullivan's *Mikado*—yet who to-day remembers his venture into grand opera, *Ivanhoe*?

Birds, Demons, and Dew

both in the interplanetary story and in the possibilities of voyaging to the stars. So far, there was no other science fiction. The robot, the Time Machine, the mutant, and the death-ray were not to make their bow until much later. The next effort was still concerned with the space theme, and was by no less a person than Cyrano de Bergerac, that curious figure who has been regarded variously as a hero, a potentially brilliant writer of verse, a charlatan, and a buffoon. Cyrano is best remembered to-day as the possesser of a flashing sword and a peculiarly long nose, but in fact he has a greater claim to fame. He was the first to suggest space-travel by means of what we now term the principle of reaction.

Cyrano's several voyages made use of a number of ingenious methods of propulsion. The first involved not demons or gansas, but simply dew. His reasoning was straightforward enough. The Sun seems to suck up dew; therefore a man who carried enough bottles of dew about his person should be sucked up with them, and if properly aimed and guided ought to finish up on the Moon. His first effort proved unsuccessful, since he became alarmed at his rate of ascent and started to smash his dew-bottles, with the unfortunate result that he fell back to Earth and landed in Canada. His second attempt, involving a flying chariot, met with equal ill-fortune, and he landed heavily on the ground, bruising himself in the process. Then, by some mischance, he found that a party of soldiers had discovered his chariot and that fire-crackers were being fastened to it. Cyrano, furious, leaped into the chariot, and as soon as the fire-crackers went off he soared up into the air and departed in a blaze of sparks. When the crackers burned out the chariot fell back to the ground, but Cyrano himself continued his journey, because he had daubed his bruises with "the marrow of animals," and this marrow was sucked up by the waning Moon.

It is only one step from Cyrano's fire-cracker to Wernher von Braun's interplanetary rocket, but Cyrano himself had no idea of the implications of what he had written. He was not attempting a scientific treatise disguised as fiction, and would, in fact, have been incapable of any such thing. He was concerned with pure fantasy, and he would have been astounded to learn that he had hit upon the vital truth that rockets, and only rockets, can carry men across the void.

There is, of course, a good reason for this. A balloon, an aeroplane, or even a jet engine depends upon air; and of the quarter-million-mile gap between Earth and Moon, all but the first few miles are virtually airless. Consequently we must find some form of propulsion which is self-supporting, and does not need air to push against or to use in any other way. The rocket is such a form; it works by 'reaction,' or by pushing against itself, just as a truck will roll when a man stands on the end of it and jumps off, thus kicking it away. Cyrano may have realized this in a vague sort of way, but certainly not clearly enough for him to put his ideas into words.

There are plenty of amusing episodes in Cyrano's *Voyages to the Moon and Sun*. We learn how he met Domingo Gonzales, who became his companion and guide so long as he stayed on the Moon, and how he went on to the Sun, landing on a sunspot and encountering talking trees, Protean men, and symbolical rivers. But on the whole his descriptions are less fascinating than Godwin's, and only one point stands out as being wholly original.

At home, Cyrano had always affirmed that the Moon must be inhabited, and had met with scorn and ridicule. When he landed on the lunar surface he was equally emphatic that the Earth is inhabited—with the result that he met with even greater scorn, almost ending in disaster when he was tried for the 'heresy' of teaching that so hostile a world as the Earth could possibly harbour intelligent life. Evidently Gonzales had not convinced his hosts of his origin, or else the friendly Prince Irdonzur was no longer in evidence. At any rate, Cyrano's reception was very different from those of

Gonzales and Duracotus, and he had difficulty in persuading the Moon-Men that he was human at all.

In a later story Cyrano developed the idea of rocket propulsion, and on the whole it is rather surprising that he was not imitated by other writers. But enough has been said to show the general trend of science fiction in the seventeenth century. Fact was being mixed with fancy; there was an increasing tendency to keep to what was thought to be fact, and only in the actual mode of propulsion did the storytellers resort to the fantastic.

In 1752 the famous French writer Voltaire published a curious book, *Micromégas*, in which we first come across the notion of an extra-terrestrial being visiting the Earth. Of course, the Levanian demons conjured up by Fiolxhilda could cross the "bridge of shadow" during an eclipse, but Micromégas himself was not bothered by a journey of a mere quarter of a million miles. He hailed from Sirius, the Dog-Star, and was a giant both in body and mind. Since Sirius is a vast star, Micromégas was a vast being who regarded a terrestrial whale as microscopic. After writing a book considered to be heretical, he was condemned to leave his Sirian home for eight hundred years, which to him must have been the equivalent of a month or two by our standards, and he decided to carry out a grand tour of the universe, which he apparently managed to do without resorting to anything so crude as a space-ship. He visited both Earth and the planet Saturn, and found it hard to believe that the tiny wriggling beings that he saw upon our world could be possessed of true reasoning power. Pausing only to lunch lightly by swallowing up a couple of mountains, he went his way.

Already we can see a marked distinction between our Types 1 and 2. Lucian's *True History* and Voltaire's *Micromégas* were of Type 1; to them, science mattered not a jot—and the same applies to Cyrano, even if he did make some brilliant guesses. Kepler's book was of Type 2, since he was quite prepared to believe in demons, and his lunar picture was as accurate as he could make it; Godwin's *Man in the Moone* was a borderline case. At all events these early stories, apart, in places, from the *Somnium*, were pleasant enough. There was as yet no tendency to regard science fiction as the undesirable offspring of true literature.

3

THE GENIUS OF VERNE

THE interest aroused by the works of Kepler, Godwin, and Cyrano was hardly maintained during the eighteenth and early nineteenth centuries. A few books appeared which can legitimately be classed as science fiction, but their circulation was very limited, and to-day they are almost forgotten. At last, in 1865, came two works of the greatest importance—Jules Verne's *From the Earth to the Moon* and Achille Eyraud's *Voyage to Venus*.

Both Verne and Eyraud were Frenchmen, and both possessed the gift of lively imagination, but there the resemblance ended. Eyraud was, frankly, mediocre as a writer, and his book was never reprinted, so that it is now extremely scarce; I have been unable to track down a copy of it, and the only reliable reference is made in a book by the great astronomer Camille Flammarion (*Les Mondes Imaginaires et les Mondes Réels*). Verne, on the other hand, is almost as well-known to-day as he was during his lifetime. He wrote dozens of books which still make fascinating reading, and one cannot avoid being thrilled by the "Extraordinary Travels" which flowed from his pen as water flows from a tap. Each one is different; each one has an allure of its own; and in addition to his descriptive powers Verne was also a master of characterization.

Altogether, he wrote three stories of an interplanetary nature. *From the Earth to the Moon* was followed some years later by its sequel, *Round the Moon*, and later still came *Hector Servadac*. For all intents and purposes the first two books can be classed together as one long novel, though the third is entirely separate and not nearly so good.

Jules Verne was born at Nantes, on the River Loire, on February 8, 1828. His father was a serious-minded, eminently respectable lawyer, and he had every intention of making his son follow in his footsteps. Jules had other ideas. Even as a ten-year-old boy his imagination had begun to show itself, and so had the urge to travel. His first attempt ended rather unhappily. One morning he crept out of the house and made his way to the waterfront, where the *Coralie*, a three-masted ocean-going ship, lay at anchor preparing to start on a voyage to the Indies. Somehow or other he managed to bribe a cabin-boy to change places with him, and when the *Coralie* sailed Jules sailed with it. It was not long before his parents found out what had happened, and when the ship called in at the port of Paimbœuf on the same evening Verne senior was there to meet it. Jules' voyage ended there and then with a sound caning and a spell on bread and water, but the wish to travel remained. It is perhaps rather strange that in his later life, when he was world-famous and had no financial worries, he never did roam about as he might have been expected to do. However, his travels in imagination carried him not only over the whole planet, but even beyond it.

At the age of twenty he was sent off to Paris to begin his legal studies. Fortunately he was quite unable to take the finer points of law seriously, and he spent most of his time writing magazine stories and plays, one or two of which were even published. Always he longed for books, and on one occasion he lived on dried prunes for three days in order to save up enough money to buy a well-bound edition of Shakespeare. Things were not easy for him, and he discovered to his cost that one cannot survive wholly upon a diet of literature. "The cotton socks that I am wearing at the moment are like a spider's web in which a hippopotamus has been in residence," he wrote to his father. "Even my Uncle Prudent, who is truly remarkable in this same respect, hasn't a single pair that can touch mine for holes. Never, in fact, have holes multiplied with such astonishing fecundity.

The reality still clings about my calves, but my feet tread the void!"

His first stroke of really good fortune came when he succeeded in obtaining the appointment of Secretary of the Théâtre Lyrique. At about the same time he married, and to help make ends meet he joined a firm in the Paris equivalent of the Stock Exchange. Any thoughts of a legal career were definitely abandoned, but as yet he was still comparatively unknown; the Extraordinary Travels had not begun.

One essay produced by Verne during this period is of particular interest. It was concerned with Edgar Allan Poe, the strange genius of American literature. Verne sang Poe's praises as a creator of the eerie and the supernatural, but he added a significant criticism. One of Poe's works was *The Unparalleled Adventure of Hans Pfaall*, published in 1835, in which the hero travels to the Moon by means of a balloon. Jules Verne pointed out that Poe had robbed his story of realism by making use of an obviously impossible method of travel, since even in those days it was known that any talk of interplanetary ballooning was sheer nonsense. It is true that Poe did not mean his story to be taken seriously, but the fault was there. "Why," Verne asked in effect, "did not Poe take the trouble to correct his science? His story would have lost nothing, and gained much."

It was this critical attitude that made Verne great. Even with the most light-hearted of his Voyages he always tried to keep his facts within the bounds of reason, and he was no dabbler in fiction of the bug-eyed monster and ray-gun type. Naturally he made mistakes, and occasionally he made unwarrantable assumptions, but on the whole he succeeded wonderfully well, and he may be regarded as the real founder of genuine Type 2 science fiction. It is easier to believe in Verne's space-gun than in H. G. Wells's gravity-screening material. Neither is practicable, but the one is scientific while the other is not.

In 1861 Jules Verne and his friend Hignard set out upon

a sea-trip to Norway, and on their return sighted Iceland, which was later to be the starting-point of one of Verne's best stories. He arrived home just before the birth of his only child, a boy. Verne's love for his son could not be doubted, but the crying baby unsettled him, and he spent a good deal of his time during the next year or so at a club for science writers. It was here that he met Félix Tournachon, better known under his pseudonym of Nadar, who was one of the most popular men of the Paris of the sixties.

Nadar was deeply interested in aerial flight, and he discussed his ideas with Verne, infecting him with similar enthusiasm. Each tackled the problem according to his own capabilities. Nadar, the practical man, actually built his vast balloon *Géant*, and flew it; Verne's equally famous *Victoria* existed on paper only, but was little the worse for that. While Nadar planned, Verne wrote. The result was the first of his Travels, *Five Weeks in a Balloon*.

It seems that Verne had almost despaired of making his name as a writer, and it is related that on one occasion he flung his manuscripts on to the fire, so that all of them would have been destroyed but for the promptness of his wife in pulling them out again. It seemed to him that he was always too late with his ideas, and he wrote to his father in a spirit of bitterness: "Even if I discovered a new planet, I believe it would at once explode, just to prove me wrong." But in the late autumn of 1862 he visited a Paris publisher, Hetzel, with his latest story, and this proved to be the turning-point in his literary career.

Hetzel, a progressive publisher, was always more than glad to discover a new writer of talent. He had some comments to make upon Verne's manuscript; Verne revised it, and this time Hetzel was overjoyed. *Five Weeks in a Balloon* was clearly outstanding, and publisher and author signed a contract without delay. Verne was to produce two books a year for twenty years, or, alternatively, forty books in a shorter period of time.

Jules Verne was in the seventh heaven of delight. He

resigned his position on the Exchange, and parts of his farewell speech are worth remembering: "I have just written a novel in a new form, one that is entirely my own. If it succeeds I shall have stumbled upon a gold-mine. In that case I shall go on writing and writing without pause, while you others will go on buying shares the day before they drop and selling them the day before they rise. I am leaving the Exchange. Good evening, *mes enfants!*" Duquesnel, who was present at the time and wrote an article about it forty years later, added: "Did the group really take this declaration seriously? It scarcely matters. Verne was speaking the truth. . . . An unknown writer of genius had created the scientific novel."[1]

Nadar's balloon created a stir when it made its first ascent from the Champ-de-Mars, but the sensation made by Verne's book was probably even greater. It was a triumphant success; it was read not only by schoolboys, for whom it was originally intended, but also by their parents, and before long it had been translated into all European and most other languages. Its theme is summed up in his sub-title, "A Voyage of Discovery and Adventure in Central Africa." The story of how Dr Samuel Fergusson and his companions drifted over the Dark Continent is not real science fiction, but the scientific tendency is plain, and Hetzel pressed the young author for a second work on the same lines. Verne was only too ready to comply, and from that moment onward he wrote book after book, all refreshingly original and all of high literary quality.

The first pure science fiction from his pen came two years later, with the *Journey to the Centre of the Earth*. In my personal view, for what it is worth, this book is one of the best that Verne ever wrote. I may be prejudiced by the fact that it was the first that I read (at the age of nine), but its appeal is irresistible, and the plot is worth describing.

The story begins with Professor Otto Lidenbrock, a

[1] These two quotations are given in Marguerite Allotte de la Fuÿe's admirable book *Jules Verne*.

German mineralogist, who discovers an ancient Runic document written by the sixteenth-century alchemist Arne Saknussemm. Axel, the professor's nephew, deciphers it as follows: "Descend the crater of Snæfells Jokul, on which the shadow of Scartaris falls before the kalends of July, bold explorer, and you will reach the centre of the Earth. I have done it." Snæfells is an extinct volcano in Iceland, the island that Verne had glimpsed during his voyage with Hignard, and Lidenbrock is quick to realize that the correct crater must be the one indicated by the midday shadow of Scartaris, one of the several peaks of the mountain. Without delay, he and Axel set off. Accompanied by an Icelander, Hans Bjelke, they lower themselves down the immense orifice and begin what Axel describes as "the real journey."

Verne is not content with a story made up simply of geological speculation. In their wanderings below the Earth's crust the explorers discover a subterranean sea in which live plesiosaurs and ichthyosaurs, those terrifying marine monsters which flourished above ground during the Mesozoic Era; a petrified forest; a human skull; and, last but not least, a herd of living mastodons in charge of a being "more than twelve feet high; his head, as big as that of a buffalo, half hidden in his wild locks ... He was brandishing in his hand an enormous bough—a worthy crook for this antediluvian shepherd!" But the story-teller is too skilful to afford his voyagers anything but a fleeting glimpse of the stranger, and the reader is left in doubt as to whether Lidenbrock and Axel really saw it or not. Finally, the explorers return to the surface by being hurled forth from the vent of an active volcano, Stromboli.

Nowadays it is known that no such voyage is possible. The Earth is not a cool, solid body throughout; as one descends, the temperature rises by about one degree Fahrenheit for every fifty feet down. It is true that the temperature gradient is not constant, and that the central temperature is probably only a few thousands of degrees, but studies of earthquake waves have shown that there is a central core, perhaps four

The Genius of Verne

thousand miles in diameter, that must be in virtually a liquid state. Any form of life at great depths is as out of the question, as is Lidenbrock's subterranean sea.

The origin of the Earth is still wrapped in mystery. Formerly the answer given was that our planet, and its companion worlds, were drawn off the Sun by the tidal action of a passing star, but nowadays this attractive theory has had to be given up, and it is more probable that the Earth was born out of matter collected by the Sun as it plunged through an interstellar 'cloud.' At any rate, the young Earth was extremely hot. Some of that heat remains; and though the central core is not so violently heated as used to be thought, it is still far from cold.

Earthquakes may be destructive, but they have their uses from a scientific point of view. When a shock occurs it sets up three types of waves in the Earth's body—surface waves, 'push waves,' similar to those set up when a solid rod is tapped at one end, and 'shake waves,' similar to those set up in a mat when one end is shaken. Both the push waves and shake waves will travel through a solid, but only the push waves can pass through a liquid; the shake waves are cut off. Since the shake waves cannot pass through the Earth's core, we can only assume that this core is in a condition not unlike that of a liquid.

We can thus draw up a reasonable picture of how the Earth is built. The crust itself, 40 to 50 miles thick, is composed of rocks, mainly granite below and sediments above. Below the crust is a layer made up largely of a rock called peridotite, 600 miles thick, and below this again is a layer of stony material extending down to 2000 miles, after which we come to the main core. This core seems to be made up chiefly of iron or nickel-iron, though there are still some features of it which remain unexplained.

Yet little of this was known when Verne wrote his story. Sir Humphry Davy, one of the greatest scientists of the nineteenth century, held different views. He believed the Earth to be made up in much the way described by Verne's travellers, and, indeed, Verne was careful to quote Davy's views in the first section of his novel. He was quite within his rights in selecting the theory which would lead to the best story, particularly with the backing of a man like Davy. A trip from Snæfells to Stromboli by means of underground travel seemed, in fact, to be far from an impossibility.

The book proved to be an even greater success than *Five Weeks in a Balloon* and the rest of Verne's early tales. Encouraged by this, the story-teller decided to venture farther afield. From going downwards, he would go upward. He would visit the Moon.

It was inevitable that Jules Verne, with his fertile mind and vivid imagination, should turn to the interplanetary story sooner or later; but, as usual, he was wise enough to keep a tight rein upon his pen. Demons, waterspouts, and gansas were not for him, and neither would he make use of the balloon, as Poe had done. He was left with only two possibilities—the space-gun and the rocket. He selected the former, and although this was a serious mistake, he took care to ensure that all details of construction and operation were as accurate as possible.

The first special point concerned the speed at which the projectile would have to leave the mouth of the cannon. Verne fixed this at seven miles a second, and he had sound reasons for so doing. Most people of to-day—certainly most boys—are familiar with the term 'escape velocity,' but the principle is so important that it is worth considering in more detail.

Gravity holds us to the Earth. It is a force which we do not really understand; we know, however, how it acts, and Sir Isaac Newton, in his immortal *Principia*, worked out the manner in which every body attracts every other. A massive body has more attractive power than an inferior one, and Nevil Maskelyne, once Astronomer Royal, used the pull of the Scottish mountain Schiehallion to 'weigh' the Earth. He measured the amount by which the mountain deflected

The Genius of Verne

a weight hung on the end of a plumb-line, calculated the density of the material making up the mountain, and arrived at a very reasonable figure for the mass of the whole planet. Clearly the Earth, with its tremendous mass, must have an extremely powerful pull.

But though the Earth's tug is strong, it is not infinitely strong. A simple experiment will prove this. If I throw a penny into the air, it will rise to a certain height and then fall back to the ground; if I give it a greater starting velocity it will rise to a greater altitude before dropping back. Disregarding air resistance for the moment, we can picture a penny being hurled upward with a starting velocity of seven miles a second. In this case it will reach an infinite altitude; in other words, it will never come down. The Earth will not be able to pull it back, and the penny will escape into space, to become a tiny independent particle. This is why seven miles a second is termed the Earth's escape velocity.

It is now clear why Verne gave his projectile this speed. If the projectile had started more slowly, it would have fallen back to the ground, but at seven miles a second it would be perfectly capable of reaching the Moon. Verne explained all this in the first two chapters of his book, putting the words into the mouth of Impey Barbicane, president of the Baltimore Gun Club:

> "I have looked at the question in all its aspects, and from my indisputable calculations it results that any projectile, hurled at an initial speed of seven miles a second,[1] and directed at the Moon, must necessarily reach her. I have, therefore, the honour of proposing to you, my worthy colleagues, the attempting of this little experiment."

The Gun Club itself was a typical Verne creation. It had been formed during the American Civil War by a group of artillerymen, and consisted largely of men whose experiments had resulted in their being forced to use "crutches, wooden

---

[1] The original book naturally uses the Metric system.

legs, articulated arms, hands with hooks, gutta-percha jaws, silver craniums, platinum noses.... It was calculated that in the Gun Club there was not quite one arm among every four persons, and only two legs amongst six." The end of the war was almost a disaster for the artillerymen. They were left with "nothing whatever to do," and the idea of firing a shot to the Moon came as a most welcome diversion. It was planned to make the projectile nine feet in diameter and to fire it from the mouth of a giant cannon to be called the "Columbiad." The explosive was to be gun-cotton, with the projectile itself made of aluminium, then a rare and very costly metal.

Then came a dramatic development. Michel Ardan, a young Frenchman, not only volunteered to go to the Moon inside the projectile, but reconciled Impey Barbicane with his mortal enemy, Captain Nicholl, and persuaded them to accompany him. The form of the projectile was altered. It became cylindro-conical, and was fitted with hydraulic shock-absorbers, an air-conditioning plant, padded walls with deeply set windows, and other refinements to be found in any modern space-ship design.

The cannon itself was a 900-feet-deep vertical barrel, weighing 68,040 tons. It was packed with 400,000 pounds of gun-cotton, and cost 5,446,675 dollars, a sum raised by voluntary contributions. The first book, *From the Earth to the Moon*, deals simply with the preparations for the great experiment, and ends on a note of high drama when the powder is fired and the projectile, bearing Ardan, Barbicane, and Nicholl, "cleaves the air amidst the flaming smoke."

One of the greatest merits of the story is the way in which it is written. Verne's dry, attractive sense of humour is probably more in evidence than in any of his other books; Barbicane, Ardan, Captain Nicholl—all are beautifully drawn characters. Barbicane is

> a great caster of projectiles, and Nicholl an equally great forger of plate-armour.... As soon as Barbicane had invented

a new projectile, Nicholl invented a new plate-armour. The President of the Gun Club passed his life in piercing holes, the Captain in preventing him from doing it. Hence a constant rivalry which even touched their persons. Nicholl appeared in Barbicane's dreams as an impenetrable ironclad against which he split, and Barbicane in Nicholl's dreams appeared like a projectile which ripped him up.

Finally the two agreed to a duel, in which they were to "stalk" each other with guns through a dense wood. Michel Ardan, going in search of them, found them both forgetful of their wish for vengeance. Nicholl was busily engaged in releasing a bird which had become entangled in a spider's web, while Barbicane was equally immersed in working out the details of the projectile's shock-absorbers.

Ardan himself was a pen-portrait of Félix Tournachon, and the name is, of course, an obvious anagram of Nadar. He was the first of science fiction's true space-heroes, and his attitude was summed up in his reply to a question as to how he would return from the Moon once he had reached it. He said, simply, "I shall not come back." It must, of course, be remembered that when Verne wrote his story, ninety years ago, the hostile and airless nature of the Moon was not fully appreciated.

One of the prophetic touches of humour in the book concerned the raising of money for the experiment. According to Verne, every country in the world contributed something —apart from England. The British received the news of the Gun Club's plan with "contemptuous apathy," and "did not subscribe a single farthing." In our own century space-travel has become a real possibility, and yet the British in general held rocket science in equal contempt until the rain of German V2's during the War awoke the slumbering Government departments with an unpleasant jump. Even jet propulsion had been dismissed as totally impracticable, and in a famous letter written to the British Interplanetary Society in 1934 the Under-Secretary of State for Air said that although work in other countries was being followed with interest, "scientific investigation into the possibilities has given no indication that this method can be a serious competitor to the airscrew-engine combination. We do not consider that we should be justified in spending any time or money on it ourselves."[1] That particular official was indeed a logical descendant of the Englishman pictured by Jules Verne. Even more recently, in January 1956, Dr Woolley, the Astronomer Royal, has observed that the idea of interplanetary flight is "utter bilge" and "rather rot." It is worth recalling that only a few years before Orville Wright's first ascent Professor Newcomb, an eminent American astronomer, proved conclusively that flight in a heavier-than-air machine was out of the question.

Since the Gun Club's projectile would never return to Earth, it was essential to watch it during its journey through space. The only way of doing this was to build a giant telescope, and Verne planned one with a mirror 192 inches across, to be set up on the summit of Long's Peak.

Astronomical telescopes are of two types, refractors and reflectors. The refracting type, invented in 1608 by Hans Lippersheim and first turned to the heavens by Galileo in the following year, collects light by means of a lens known as an object glass, while the reflector, developed later in the seventeenth century by Sir Isaac Newton, dispenses with the object glass and collects light by means of a mirror. What happens is that in the reflecting telescope the light from the star, or whatever object is being examined, passes down an open tube until it hits the mirror at the bottom; this mirror is curved so as to reflect the light back up the tube, where it is directed to the side of the instrument by means of a smaller mirror, and is then viewed through a magnifying eyepiece.[2] Each type of instrument has its own advantages and drawbacks, but Verne's reasons for preferring the reflector were

---

[1] Quoted in P. E. Cleator's admirable book *Into Space* (London, 1953).
[2] This is the Newtonian arrangement; there are others.

The Genius of Verne

perfectly sound. A large mirror is far easier to make than a large lens, and all the world's most powerful telescopes are therefore reflectors.

In 1865 the largest telescope in existence was that at Parsonstown, in Ireland, owned by the Earl of Rosse. The mirror was 72 inches across, and Lord Rosse had used it to make observations of great scientific importance. The idea of building an instrument with a 192-inch mirror seemed fantastic. Yet only eighty years later the 200-inch reflector of Palomar Mountain was almost complete; it has in fact, been said that the Palomar telescope is almost the twin of the Gun Club's. Note, too, that the 200-inch is erected at a height of several thousands of feet above sea-level. The Earth's atmosphere is a handicap to the astronomer, since it is dirty and turbulent, and the performance of a telescope is improved out of all recognition if it can be built above the lowest and densest layers of air. It would indeed have been a striking prophecy had Verne selected Palomar as his site instead of Long's Peak, as he might well have done.

Round the Moon, the sequel to Verne's first book, takes up the story from the moment at which the projectile leaves the Earth. Almost at once the adventurers meet with danger in the shape of

> an enormous disk, the colossal dimensions of which could not be estimated. Its face turned towards the Earth was brilliantly lighted. It looked like a small moon reflecting the light of the large one. It advanced at a prodigious speed, and seemed to describe round the Earth an orbit right across the passage of the projectile. To the movement of translation was added a movement of rotation upon itself. . . . The asteroid passed at a distance of a few hundred yards from the projectile and disappeared, not so much on account of the rapidity of its course, but because its side opposite to the Moon was suddenly confronted with the absolute darkness of space.

Verne had, in fact, pictured a minor earth satellite, circling our world at a distance of some six thousand miles. The idea is not so fantastic as it sounds. A minor satellite of this sort was actually thought to exist, and even to-day an energetic search is being made for a body of such a nature. If a second satellite exists it must, of course, be very small, but in 1954 Dr Clyde Tombaugh, discoverer of the planet Pluto, began to look for it with the aid of all the instruments developed by modern science. Whether or not he will be successful remains to be seen; but as he and other eminent astronomers take the idea seriously, we can hardly blame Jules Verne for taking up a similar attitude.

Actually, the asteroid played an important part in the story. It pulled the projectile out of its calculated path, so that instead of landing on the Moon, Barbicane and his companions swung round in a vast, sweeping movement before returning to the "neutral point" where the terrestrial and lunar pulls balance each other. When they arrived back at this point, Barbicane fired the projectile's rockets, and the force of recoil caused the projectile itself to pass beyond the sphere of lunar attraction, so that it fell back to Earth and landed in the Pacific Ocean. The journey round the Moon is vividly described. Verne consulted the best surface map available at the time, Beer and Mädler's, and his account of what the travellers saw of the Earth-turned hemisphere is perfectly accurate. His method of dealing with the hidden hemisphere is, however, even more interesting.

We know that the Moon revolves round the Earth in the same time that it takes to turn upon its own axis, so that there is a part of its surface which we can never see. An amateur Shakespeare summed matters up rather neatly in the following rhyme:[1]

> O Moon, lovely Moon with the beautiful face,
> Careering throughout the bound'ries of space,
> Whenever I see you, I think in my mind—
> Shall I ever, O ever, behold thy behind?

---

[1] Quoted in my *Guide to the Moon*. The authoress was, I am told, a housemaid in the service of a well-known poet. It is interesting to speculate as to whether the poet concerned felt at all jealous.

The Genius of Verne

Although the Moon appears to wobble slightly, and we can at various times examine four-sevenths of its disk, the remaining three-sevenths will remain unexplored until the interplanetary rockets (or cameras) start to fly. An old theory, due to the Danish astronomer Hansen, supposed that all the lunar air and water had been drawn round to the hidden hemisphere, making part of the Moon habitable. Nowadays this idea has been shown to be false, and there can be no doubt that the averted area is much the same as the area we can see; but Verne used the "Hansonian Moon" to excellent advantage.

As Barbicane, Ardan, and Captain Nicholl passed round the unknown hemisphere, it was night-time below, so that they could make out nothing but blackness. Their one glimpse was afforded them when a meteor burst into flame near by, and for a few precious seconds they saw "long bands across the disk, veritable clouds formed in a very restricted atmospheric medium. . . . The immense tracts, no longer arid plains, but veritable seas, oceans which reflected in their liquid mirror all the fires of space." Again we are left in doubt as to whether the vision was imagination or reality, and we are reminded of the strange creatures seen by Professor Lidenbrock deep down near the centre of the Earth.

The science in Verne's story is maintained to the very end. When the projectile fell eventually into the sea the members of the Gun Club chartered a ship and went out to fish it up from the ocean bed. Yet they all forgot that while the projectile displaced twenty-eight tons of water, it weighed only ten tons—and consequently it floated! When the voyagers were found they were seated inside their spacecraft enjoying a quiet game of dominoes.

Clearly Verne had given a great deal of thought to the problems of how to make his tale plausible, and some of his forecasts were amazingly accurate. He even introduced rocket power, and on the whole it is surprising that he did not make use of it for the whole trip. When *Round the Moon* was published, in 1870, there seemed, however, to be no valid reason why a real Barbicane should not make the journey at some date in the not too distant future. Even in 1956 space-guns still have their supporters, but it is now known that there are two major obstacles which prove fatal to the whole idea.

The first of these is the heat set up by friction. Air is comparatively dense, and a solid body moving through it at seven miles a second would promptly become so hot that it would vaporize. Practical proof is provided by meteors, or shooting-stars. These are small pieces of matter, revolving round the Sun like miniature planets, and are very numerous in space. If a meteor comes close to the Earth, and is moving in the right direction at the right speed, it may be drawn downward by the gravitational pull of our world, so that it enters the atmosphere. Below a height of 120 miles the friction increases rapidly; the meteor becomes first warm and then hot, finally bursting into flame and burning itself away in a streak of fire. The average shooting-star is a tiny thing, smaller than a grain of rice, though occasionally we meet giants which survive the complete drop and are found later as 'meteorites.'

The air-density at 120 miles, where meteors first become luminous, is a very small fraction of the density close to the Earth's surface. If Verne's Columbiad had been fired in Florida, as planned, the projectile would have been vaporized even before it had left the mouth of the gun, and Barbicane, Nicholl, and Michel Ardan would have been vaporized with it.

There is another obstacle to be faced, different in character but equally troublesome. As every one knows, the sudden ascent of a violent electric lift gives a distinct jar to its passengers, and gives rise to the feeling that one's knees are about to hit one's chin. The human body is, in fact, a frail piece of mechanism, and a sudden departure at escape velocity would have consequences that would be unfortunate, to put it mildly. Neglecting air resistance, Barbicane

The Genius of Verne

and his companions might indeed have reached the Moon; but they would have reached it in the form of fine jelly spread against the walls of their projectile, and would thus have been in no fit state to carry out scientific research.

Verne did not realize either of these limitations. Had he done so he would have taken them into account, particularly since he did not fail to appreciate the power of the rocket. Nevertheless, it is hard to blame him. His story was correct with regard to scientific knowledge of his time, and it was many years before the space-gun was definitely shown to be impracticable. Both Hermann Oberth and Guido von Pirquet, the twentieth-century rocket pioneers, thought it worth while to investigate the possibilities of building a space-gun on top of a peak and then evacuating the barrel of the cannon, each of which precautions would reduce air-resistance. They concluded that even so, the heat generated would be fatal; but if they were initially uncertain about it, it is not surprising that Verne fell into the same trap. So far as I know, the last noteworthy space-gun story was written by an electrical engineer, E. F. Northrup, as recently as 1937. It was called *Zero to Eighty*, and described a projectile launched from a 200-kilometre ramp built up the slopes to Mount Popocatepetl, the object of the ramp being to allow the projectile to build up speed gradually. The book even included a forty-page mathematical appendix!

The only other bad mistake in Verne's *Round the Moon* concerns that vexed spot the 'neutral point,' where the Earth's gravity balances that of the Moon. It was said that as the projectile drew away from the Earth, the travellers gradually lost "weight" until by the time they reached the neutral point they no longer weighed anything at all: "Their heads vacillated on their shoulders. Their feet no longer kept at the bottom of the projectile. . . . Suddenly Michel, making a slight spring, left the floor and remained suspended in the air." As they passed the neutral point, and fell towards the Moon, their weight returned.

This is incorrect. Actually, Barbicane and his companions would have been weightless from the time that they left the barrel of the Columbiad, as can be shown by means of a simple experiment. If a penny is placed on a postcard, it naturally presses upon the card; but if the two are dropped, they fall at the same speed in the same direction, and until they hit the carpet the penny ceases to press upon the card. It is, in fact, weightless with reference to the card. Similarly, the lunar travellers would have been weightless with reference to the projectile, since they and it would have been moving in the same path.

Conditions of this sort are known as 'free fall,' with zero gravity. Weightlessness has nothing to do with passing beyond the Earth's gravity field, as is often supposed, since the terrestrial pull extends, in theory, to infinity. Bound to the Earth as we are, we cannot subject ourselves to zero gravity, but airmen screaming towards the ground in a steep dive can experience a momentary sensation of it. I have done so myself.

The neutral point is thus of no importance whatsoever; moreover, it is only the spot where the terrestrial and lunar pulls become equal, and the pull of the Sun has still to be reckoned with. But even though Verne made a mistake in this connexion, he was on the right track, since he did at least take loss of weight into account.

From the Earth to the Moon and its sequel have been worth describing in some detail, because when taken together they form one of the most important science-fiction books ever written. Popular interest was really aroused, and no one could doubt that the scientific novel had come to stay. In 1870, the same year that *Round the Moon* appeared, Verne produced the book that is generally regarded as his masterpiece—*Twenty Thousand Leagues under the Sea*. He was also awarded the Légion d'Honneur, and this proved to be one of the last decorations given by the Royal House of France. War with Prussia had broken out. Jules Verne served as a coastguard—he was never happier than when afloat—and when the disastrous conflict was over it took both Verne and his publisher many months to pick up the threads once more.

Verne was now over forty, and he spent most of the rest of his long life quietly in Amiens, pouring out book after book. Some were novels of adventure, such as *Round the World in Eighty Days;* others were definite science fiction, such as *The Purchase of the Pole,* in which Barbicane, Nicholl, and Michel Ardan reappear in order to try to change the inclination of the Earth's axis by the recoil of an enormous cannon tunnelled into the side of Mount Kilimanjaro. *The Clipper of the Clouds*, published in 1886, describes a heavier-than-air flying machine, and might well have been regarded as fantasy at the time when it was written.

The other interplanetary novel from Verne's pen was written in 1877. In *Hector Servadac* he describes how a comet grazes the Earth, scoops up Hector and his servant, and carries them round the Solar System. As they explore the comet they come across other pieces of the Earth which have been taken up in the collision, and upon one of these, part of the Rock of Gibraltar, they find two Englishmen who had been playing chess when the disaster occurred, and were so absorbed in their game that they were quite unaware of anything unusual. It cannot be claimed that *Hector Servadac* is one of Verne's better stories, and it is far inferior to *Round the Moon*, but it has at least the merit of being original.

Jules Verne died in 1905, mourned and honoured by countless folk in every country in the world. He is one of the great figures of French literature, and as a story-teller he has probably never been equalled. It is not correct to say that he created the scientific novel, but he certainly developed it in its modern form, and his influence is so strong that it is difficult to evaluate. Had he resorted to the tricks of the lesser writer, and introduced strange beings on other worlds, he would have been of minor importance; but his attention to detail, his insistence upon correct science, and his dry sense of humour, which never descends to the ridiculous, lift him head and shoulders above his imitators.

Had Verne's successors followed the methods used in his "Extraordinary Travels," science fiction would never have acquired the evil reputation that clings to it to-day.

4

H. G. WELLS

Though it is sometimes said that H. G. Wells was the English Verne, no two men could have been less alike, and to compare them is unfair to both. From a purely literary point of view Wells's influence was probably greater than Verne's, but nearly all his science-fiction stories were written early in his career, and in later life he more or less abandoned them.

Wells is so definitely a figure of modern times that it is not easy to realize that his public life overlapped that of Verne, who is so much a figure of the past. The two men never met; it is interesting to speculate as to how they would have reacted had such a meeting been possible. Actually, the first of Wells's interplanetary novels, *The War of the Worlds*, appeared in 1898, while Verne was still actively at work, but it is improbable that the creator of the "Extraordinary Travels" ever read it. Three years later, in 1901, Wells produced *The First Men in the Moon*. And that was more or less the end of his career as an interplanetary author, though a good many more of his stories, both short and long, can be classed under the general heading of science fiction.

Herbert George Wells, born in 1866, was educated at Midhurst Grammar School. He took his Bachelor of Science degree at college, and taught for a time, but he never pretended to have any great scientific ability. Indeed, one has the impression that pure science bored him. He was interested mainly in its effects upon human society, and this may be why he drew up his plots in a way which would have been frowned upon by Verne.

Wells in his early phase was a story-teller first and a technician afterwards. To him, scientific accuracy was of secondary importance so long as the tale held together and sounded plausible. Whereas Verne had hesitated before departing from strict fact—remember how he left a doubt in the reader's mind as to the reality of Lidenbrock's antediluvian shepherd and Barbicane's lunar oceans—Wells allowed his imagination full rein. He was perfectly prepared to equip the Moon with a dense atmosphere and luxuriant vegetation, even though astronomical studies had shown that any such idea was absurd, and he was equally prepared to populate Mars with hideous monsters of unsociable inclinations. His very first story, *The Time Machine*, describes the adventures of a man who had learned how to journey at will into the future and the past; later he described a crystal "egg" which could be used as a television relay between Mars and Earth; he created a race of strange, inhuman beings who lived at the bottom of the sea. Such was his literary power that all these impossibilities seem to become possible, or even probable, as we read his words.

Some of the best of Wells's fantasies are to be found in three books made up of short tales—*The Plattner Story and Others, Tales of Space and Time*, and *Twelve Stories and a Dream*. To give anything like an adequate description of them would be out of place in the present book, but one or two examples may serve to show the general trend of his ideas. I will say nothing about *The Time Machine* for the moment, since it is not really a short story and is in any case too important to be glossed over.

The Plattner Story itself introduces the idea of a world occupying the same 'space' and 'time' as our own, but existing in a different dimension, so that it can have no communication with ours. Gottfried Plattner, an inoffensive preparatory-school master, is blown into this other world by a mild explosion during a chemistry class, and is restored nine days later by a second explosion. It is a nightmare picture that Wells paints; a picture of a shadowy, eerie existence among the strange "Watchers of the Living," unseen and unapproachable. Moreover, it is so well done that when we finish the story we are almost inclined to believe that such things might happen. Much more sinister is *The Late Mr Elvesham*, in which an old and feeble man manages to exchange his body with that of a vigorous youth —thoughtfully leaving his victim some poison in a bottle labelled "Release." *The Truth about Pyecraft* is a story of very different type, and shows Wells's great sense of humour. Pyecraft, we are told, was so concerned about his increasing fatness that he was unwise enough to swallow a villainous-tasting potion guaranteed to reduce his "weight." The result was hardly what he had expected. His fatness remained as pronounced as ever, but his physical weight decreased so rapidly that he floated up to the ceiling, where he remained until a thoughtful friend suggested the use of lead underclothing to keep him firmly anchored upon terra firma.

Few themes of modern science fiction were not anticipated by Wells. As we have seen, he did not neglect the interplanetary plot, and two of his early short stories are of particular interest. In *The Crystal Egg* he describes how an elderly naturalist discovers a glassy stone which possessed strange properties, since by looking into it one could see a curious landscape populated by winged, quasi-human creatures and lit by two moons. Wells's description of the Martian scenery is brief but graphic, and further complications are avoided by the convenient loss of the egg. The other story, *The Star*, concerns the havoc caused when a blazing sun from outer space invades the Solar System, melting the polar ice-caps and decimating mankind by causing earthquakes, tidal waves, and torrential storms. Wells does not do more than mention what he calls "the new brotherhood" which sprang up between the survivors, but we can see his social preoccupation clearly enough, and the moral of the story is obvious. He used the same theme later in his long novel *The Days of the Comet*.

The idea of a celestial collision is attractive from the

fiction-writer's point of view. Astronomically, it is by no means impossible. It is true that our planetary system is isolated in space, and that two ants flying about inside the dome of St Paul's Cathedral would be more likely to collide than are two stars, but in the universe as a whole such encounters are bound to happen now and then. The crystal egg, with its power to act as a television receiver, is much less plausible—except when described by Wells.

There can, however, be no doubt that *The First Men in the Moon*, a full-length novel first published in 1901, is fit to rank with any scientific story of yesterday or to-day. The space-ship built by Cavor, the vague, dreamy scientist who was the first of science-fiction's 'absent-minded professors,' is very different from the projectile which carried the members of the Baltimore Gun Club. It is a sphere, and it travels to the Moon not by rocket impulse or by being fired from a cannon, but because it is coated with a special substance which has the power of screening gravity.

This anti-gravity device is most tempting. If it could be made, it would solve all our space-travel problems at one stroke. Considerations of fuel and escape velocity would no longer be of any importance, and we should have to deal only with minor difficulties such as food and water storage. Wells was not the first to suggest it, since the idea had been used as long ago as 1827 in John Atterley's *Voyage to the Moon*, but he was the first to develop it in plausible form.

Cavorite, as the anti-gravity substance was named, proved to be a complete shield against the Earth's pull. As soon as its manufacture was complete, it, and everything above it, became weightless. Early in the story there is a delightful account of Cavor's first experiments, which almost ended in disaster. He completed a sheet of the marvellous substance, but at once the entire column of air above the sheet became weightless and rushed off into space. Surrounding air filled the vacuum, to be swept away in its turn, and had not the cavorite sheet itself flown upward the

H. G. Wells

experiment might have ended by removing the Earth's atmosphere altogether!

If only we can bring ourselves to believe in the principle of anti-gravity, Wells's space-ship becomes perfectly credible. By opening and shutting cavorite blinds, the scientist and his companion, Bedford, use the pull of the Moon to draw them down on to the lunar surface. Weightlessness and its effects are graphically described, and even the most unscientific of readers cannot fail to be enthralled.

The trouble about cavorite is that it is a purely imaginary substance, impossible to manufacture. The whole idea goes against everything that we have learned about nature. A mere sheet of paper will block the beam of a torch, and even the highly penetrating cosmic rays which bombard us from outer space can be stopped by sufficient thickness of lead. But gravity is due neither to waves nor to particles: it is inherent in every body, and it cannot be screened.

Even if we moved upward at seven miles a second, thus escaping from Earth, we should not be shielding ourselves from gravity. The pull would be there all the time, doing its best to drag us back, and a space-craft starting off at escape velocity would gradually slow down, coming to rest when it had reached an infinite distance. It is wrong to suppose that if we left at seven miles a second, bound for the Moon, we should continue to move at a steady seven miles a second until we arrived. If our speed remained constant in this way, the journey would take only two days. Actually, we would slacken as we drew away from Earth, and in the absence of any further application of power from the rocket motors the trip would last for five days. Counteracting gravity is not the same thing as screening it.

It is always dangerous to be dogmatic. It is, I suppose, conceivable that there is some hidden truth waiting to be discovered, and we have to admit that we still do not know just what gravity is. Judging by the available facts, however, it seems that the wonderful substance invented by Cavor must remain a pipe-dream.

The Moon-world awaiting Cavor and Bedford is very different from the volcano-scarred vista seen by Barbicane from the Columbiad projectile. As the Sun rises, the lunar atmosphere, which has remained in a frozen condition throughout the night, vaporizes in a matter of minutes; dense vegetation springs up, reminding us momentarily of Kepler's Subvolva. Not content with exploring the surface, the Earthmen even penetrate into the Moon's interior, where they find an underground world inhabited by intelligent Selenites with insect-like bodies and highly developed brains. Finally Bedford escapes and returns to Earth, while Cavor, who has injudiciously told the Selenites about the warlike habits of our own race, is kept a prisoner on the Moon.

There is plenty of food for thought here. To begin with, Wells knew perfectly well that the Moon has virtually no atmosphere, frozen or otherwise. It is easy to prove this simply by watching the Moon as it passes in front of a star; the star's light remains steady up to the moment when it is blanked out by the oncoming Moon, whereas an atmosphere surrounding the lunar edge would cause the star to flicker and fade before vanishing. More refined methods of investigation show that if there is any atmosphere at all, it cannot have a ground density of as much as $\frac{1}{10000}$ of our own, so that for all practical purposes it can be disregarded. Nor is there any mystery about this state of affairs. The Earth retains its atmospheric blanket because the escape velocity of seven miles a second is sufficient to prevent the flying air-molecules from leaking away into space. The Moon, which is far less massive than the Earth, has an escape velocity of only a mile and a half a second. Even if the Moon once possessed an air-mantle, as is quite possible, most of the molecules leaked away into space æons ago. Other worlds of similar mass, such as the planet Mercury, suffer similarly from the disadvantage of being almost airless.

Yet Wells calmly disregarded the findings of astronomy, and went so far as to cover the lunar lands with plant life,

H. G. Wells

whereas a moderate telescope suffices to show that the Moon's surface is totally barren. Moreover, it is certain that no living being could survive there, without air or water and experiencing temperatures ranging from over +200 to —250 degrees Fahrenheit, unless protected by a very efficient insulating device. This adds force to my contention that Wells was bored by science as such, and used it only as a vehicle for social studies. The last part of the book, in which Cavor gains access to a radio transmitter and sends details of lunar culture back to his home planet, is, in fact, purely social. We learn that although the Selenites are not human, they have reached a greater level of civilization than any terrestrial race.

The War of the Worlds, Wells's other great interplanetary novel, appeared three years before *The First Men in the Moon*, and here for once we have a story that is nothing more than a story. It begins with the observation of some strange spurts of flame from the disk of Mars. Some weeks later a strange missile lands in Horsell Common, near Woking, and proves to be a space-craft from the Red Planet, piloted by grotesque monsters who plan to conquer the Earth. The Martian lack of goodwill is shown in no uncertain manner when a terrestrial deputation, marching up behind a white flag of peace, is effectively toasted by an all-destroying heat-ray. Equipping themselves with mechanical Fighting Machines, the Martians soon overcome humanity's futile attempts at resistance, only to be destroyed in their turn by putrefactive and disease bacteria which their bodies are not able to combat.

The War of the Worlds is a magnificent story, told with all Wells's brilliance and power. Yet in the long run it had unhappy repercussions. It introduced the 'menace to Earth' theme which has obsessed science-fiction writers ever since, and it sowed the seeds of the popular picture of a horrific Martian. Wells's description of the unpleasant visitors leaves little to the imagination. They are bug-eyed monsters, and nothing but bug-eyed monsters; they are, in fact, the parents of all subsequent bug-eyed monsters, of which there have been many. Descriptions of the habits and customs of these beings can hardly make savoury reading, and although Wells kept up the interest without stressing the squalid and the disgusting, his less gifted disciples have been unable to do so.

It would be most unfair to say that the horror stories of later years were inspired solely by *The War of the Worlds*, but we cannot deny that Wells's book did have a bad effect inasmuch as it encouraged the unhealthy trend which has been the curse of science fiction ever since. Yet Wells himself was in no way to blame. No man is responsible for his would-be imitators.

Most of Wells's fantasies were written before the 1914 War, and after a while he lost interest in them. His later work is beyond the scope of the present discussion, even though he still produced occasional stories such as *Star Begotten* and *The Croquet Player* which might perhaps be regarded as science fiction. He lived to see the dawn of the rocket age; he died in 1946, and his passing left a gap in the literary world that is unlikely to be filled for many years, if, indeed, it can ever be wholly filled.

5

BUG-EYED MONSTERS—AND OTHERS

THE man in the street first became really space-conscious shortly after the First World War. There were very good reasons for the sudden rise in interest. Rocketry had become a serious science, the early Interplanetary Societies had been formed, and sober mathematicians such as Hermann Oberth were talking calmly about the possibilities of building space-stations and reaching the Moon.

It is true that space-travel enthusiasts were still regarded as slightly mad—for that matter, some people still think them so—but there was nothing eccentric or unscientific in the work of Professor Oberth and his colleagues. Oberth's famous book *The Rocket into Interplanetary Space* was a technical work, largely mathematical, and even though it did achieve a good deal of popularity, it was intended for the specialist, not the layman. It was published in Germany in 1923, and it was not long before attempts at practical work began both there and in America. These early experiments seem puny enough judged by modern standards. A rocket was regarded as moderately successful if it did not actually blow up while still in its launching-rack, while if it managed to fizz erratically to an altitude of a few feet it was acclaimed as outstanding. But a start had been made, and fiction-writers were not slow to take advantage of it.

It must not be thought for a moment that only Verne and Wells attempted to write science fiction between the 'classical' period, ending with Cyrano, and the beginning of the rocket era. Dozens of stories were produced, some of them, such as Greg's *Across the Zodiac* and Laszwitz's *On Two Planets*, well-written and intriguing. But these stories are best dealt with according to their particular themes, and before discussing them we must say something about the disaster that overwhelmed scientific literature between 1923 and the Second World War. This disaster took the form of a horrific, obscene creature with unsociable tendencies and a peevish disposition—the B.E.M., or Bug-Eyed Monster.

It is easy to see how the B.E.M. was able to fold all science fiction in the clammy grip of his tentacles. Oberth's book and the patient work of the amateur rocketeers marked the opening of a new age, and the planets no longer seemed impossibly distant. Authors had therefore a choice between the two kinds of story—the fantastic (Type 1), or the scientifically correct (Type 2). Mainly, and to their everlasting discredit, they chose the former. Few good stories were produced during the twenty years that preceded Hitler's war, but Type 1 tales were written in their thousands, and B.E.M.'s flourished like rats in a barn. The outbreak of hostilities mercifully killed off many of the worst space-horrors, but the damage had been done; science fiction had acquired an evil name, which still clings.

A word or two about the B.E.M., since his (or its) characteristics are vitally important in any study of science fiction. Most of the early B.E.M.'s were either Martian or Venusian,[1] with a few relatives on Mercury, the Moon, and elsewhere. They would hardly make attractive pets, as can be seen from the following description of a Martian given in a 1933 magazine:

> The creature was ovoid and horrible, with green slime dripping from its beaky nose and its cavernous mouth. The single eye was red and lustful; the grotesque lumpy body heaved and quivered as the beast lunged with its tentacles,

---

[1] There is no accepted adjective for Venus. 'Venusian' is popular, though ugly and incorrect. I have generally used the alternative 'Cytherean,' from an old name for Venus. This is equally incorrect, but seems otherwise to be an improvement. In the present book, however, I retain 'Venusian,' since this is almost always used in science fiction.

each of which terminated in a series of jagged claws itching to close upon Lorimer's flesh and crush it to pulp. The bulging, warty stomach, if stomach it can be called . . .

And so on, and so on. Lorimer, by the way, was a genial Earthman who had earned the displeasure of the Solar Police by his habit of lunching off the dwarf humanoid Mercurians. He was subsequently minced in a grinding machine. Whether his remains were then fed to the B.E.M. was not stated, but later in the story the eating habits of the Martian were described in a way which left nothing to the imagination. If I were to make extensive quotes, Her Majesty's Censor would raise strong objections—and rightly so. The magazine concerned was American, but I found it in the twopenny tray of a London bookshop, and had I not bought it (and, after perusal, burned it), some boy might easily have done so.

Clearly we are up against the obsession that all Martians, and, indeed, all interplanetary beings, are built upon this sort of pattern. Most are telepathic, and some have the ability to assume human form at will, only to revert to type at the most inconvenient moment from the hero or heroine's point of view. In one story, this time from a British-printed 'pulp' of 1936, the heroine is locked in the embrace of a handsome Jovian who changes into a leech-like monster and proceeds to suck her blood.

Why should this be so? Before we go any further it may be as well to give a brief résumé of what is in fact known about possible life on other planets, and to decide whether any B.E.M.'s can exist outside the pages of a book.

Apart from the Earth, the planets and satellites in the Solar System are not particularly welcoming. Mercury is virtually without atmosphere, and is in every respect hopelessly hostile. Of the thirty-one satellites or moons, only Titan, the sixth member of Saturn's system, has any atmosphere at all; and even Titan's air has turned out to be almost pure methane, so that it can hardly be recommended as a holiday resort. The asteroids, or minor planets, are lumps of rock with negligible gravitational pulls, and are naturally destitute of air and water. The five outer planets, Jupiter, Saturn, Uranus, Neptune, and Pluto, are bitterly cold; a heat-wave on Jupiter might send the thermometer up to a mere —200 degrees Fahrenheit, but this is somewhat chill by any standards, while Saturn and the rest are even icier. Apart from Pluto, they are, moreover, very peculiar worlds, made up chiefly of hydrogen and its compounds, and they are not 'solid' in the conventional sense of the word.

Venus is a different proposition. It is almost exactly the Earth's equal in size and mass, and lies at a mean distance of only sixty-seven million miles from the Sun, so that it may be expected to be warm. Unfortunately we know practically nothing about the surface conditions, since—unlike her mythological namesake—Venus is shy enough to hide her body beneath a mantle of impenetrable cloud or haze. Even infra-red techniques are of no use. The atmosphere itself seems to contain no free oxygen or water-vapour, but is heavily loaded with carbon dioxide, a gas which has the effect of blanketing in the Sun's heat.

We are thus reduced to guesswork. The surface is probably hot, but the exact temperature is unknown. According to one theory, Venus is a howling desert without a scrap of moisture anywhere; according to another, it is covered with water. If we adopt the marine hypothesis, it is evident that we must also agree that the carbon dioxide must have fouled the oceans, so that we can expect seas of soda-water. As has been pointed out, however, we are unlikely to find anything to mix with it, and altogether the possibilities of the existence of intelligent life on the planet do not seem to be good.

Mars is less unpleasant, and in some ways is a reasonably inviting world. It is smaller than the Earth, with a diameter of slightly over 4000 miles, and it has a less extreme temperature. The nights must be very cold, even on the equator, but a hot summer's day there can reach 80 degrees Fahrenheit. The poles are coated with a whitish deposit that is definitely ice, snow, or hoar-frost; there are also

Bug-Eyed Monsters—and Others

extensive dark tracts which are thought, though without positive proof, to be lowly vegetation. The rest of the surface is ochre in hue, and may be termed 'desert,' but the surface material cannot be sand; the colour is more probably due to the presence of reddish minerals such as felsite or limonite.

Fifty years ago it was thought that definite signs of intelligence had been detected on Mars. Linear, artificial-looking streaks stretching across the deserts, connecting dark area with dark area, were believed to be true canals, dug by Martian engineers to convey water from the icy poles to the arid temperate and equatorial regions. Unfortunately for this idea, it is now known that the polar ice-caps are extremely thin, and even if it were possible to release all the water locked up in them at one moment the result would fill only a moderate lake. Moreover, the canals themselves are not nearly so regular and artificial in appearance as the old observers believed. Under good conditions, a large telescope will show them as irregular and patchy, and it seems that they too must be made up of low-type vegetation, though their comparative straightness still remains a mystery.

The chief trouble about Mars is that its thin atmosphere lacks both oxygen and water-vapour. It seems to be made up principally of nitrogen, and the best that can be said about it is that it is not actually poisonous. Animals and even advanced plants are therefore out of the question. It is as well for me to be very definite about this, since I was badly misquoted only a year or two ago. I had been giving a public lecture in Leicester, and had made the following statement: "The lack of oxygen and water-vapour on Mars means that the vegetation, if vegetation it is, must be lowly. One would not find trees or bushes; one would not even find anything so advanced as a cabbage, and all that can be expected is something as lowly as our own lichens or mosses." The local reporter was not quite clear about this, and managed to interpret me as follows: "Mr Moore considers that the nearest terrestrial approach to life on Mars is the growth of cabbages." Even now I have not been allowed to forget the incident!

A letter written to me by an American who had read one of my books sums up the attitude of the opposition so well that it is worth quoting:

> In my view, your attitude is both narrow-minded and unscientific. I quite agree that Earthmen could not live upon Mars, or anywhere else in the Solar System, but why do you concentrate solely upon our kind of life? There may be beings differently made, who thrive in an air made up of nitrogen or pure carbon dioxide. To suggest that Man is Nature's model for all life in the universe is sheer conceit.

This sounds reasonable enough—until we come to consider the structure of matter, about which we have discovered a great deal. The crux of the problem is that there are only ninety-two naturally-occurring elements, and all matter is composed of these fundamental substances. The series is complete between 1 and 92, so that there is no chance of our having overlooked an element; one might as well try to fit a new integer between 7 and 8, or a new musical note between F-sharp and G. Only two of these elements, carbon and silicon, have any ability to build up the complex atom-groups or 'molecules' necessary for living matter. The remaining ninety elements have no such power, and any doubter can understand why if he cares to take the trouble to master a technical book on the subject (which very few doubters do). Silicon is most inferior as a molecule-builder, and all life, then, must be based upon carbon.

We must be careful to distinguish between fundamental and superficial resemblances. At first sight, for instance, there is not much in common between a jellyfish and a hippopotamus, but the two have an essential common factor: both are made up of living molecules based upon the carbon atom, and both need an equable temperature, suitable food, and a definite supply of breathable oxygen. These requirements are lacking upon Mars and Venus.

No carbon-based animals could therefore survive on these planets; and since only carbon-based life can be considered from a scientific point of view, we are justified in saying that advanced life forms on Mars and Venus simply do not exist. Which disposes, rather abruptly, of the carbon-dioxide-breathing B.E.M.

The first of the science-fiction magazine seems to have been *The Thrill Book*, edited by Harold Hersey, which was produced in New York in 1919 and ran for sixteen issues before it died. Then came *Amazing Stories*, in 1926; this was followed by others such as *Science Wonder Stories*, and then, in 1930, by *Astounding Stories of Super Science*. This last magazine is still issued, under the revised title of *Astounding Science Fiction*. It may be of interest to give the titles of the seven stories contained in its first issue:

1. The Beetle Horde.
2. The Cave of Horror.
3. Phantoms of Reality.
4. The Stolen Mind.
5. Compensation.
6. Tanks.
7. Invisible Death.

I mention *Astounding Science Fiction* partly because it was the first of the really popular science-fiction magazines, and partly because in its modern form it is among the best of them; B.E.M.'s have receded from its pages to a great extent, though they still crop up now and then, and it contains some good material, though other stories are—naturally—not so good. In September 1931 a companion magazine, *Strange Tales*, was launched. It was "dedicated to the weird and the grotesque," and died in January 1933.

If *Astounding Science Fiction* and its kind had monopolized the field there would have been no harm done, but between 1930 and the outbreak of war there arose many dozens of sensational magazines known collectively as 'pulps.' The plots of the stories in these pulps were limited in scope, and can be summed up without difficulty:

Plot No. 1. A party of travellers succeeds in reaching Mars or some other planet. The adventurers find a world inhabited by beings with many tentacles and nasty minds, and either manage to escape or (more usually) suffer a hideous death, described with ghoulish glee.

Plot No. 2. Space-explorers reach another world, to find that their brains are either controlled or disturbed by some unknown influence. Subsequently they either go mad or are converted into alien life-forms, thus suffering the same fate as their companions in Plot No. 1.

Plot No. 3. The Earth is threatened by B.E.M.'s from another planet, usually Mars. The invaders land, and show their innate lack of courtesy by using death-rays, bacteriological warfare, or mental control to decimate the population. They are then either destroyed by the hero and heroine of the story, ending their careers as putrescent puddles of slime, or else the hero and heroine manage to escape in the only remaining rocket-ship, to begin again upon some Brave New World on the far side of the galaxy.

Plot No. 4. This is more ambitious, as the action takes place upon a purely imaginary planet revolving round another star. Typical planets of this type, listed from a casual perusal of some of the pulps, are Maxarius, Marduk, Magonia, Voracia, Venomia, Plenj, and Thoss. Marduk, for example, revolves round a variable star, so that it is sometimes scorched and sometimes frozen; the people are spherical, with four legs and green slime instead of hair, while the children (should one call them Marducklings?) control the population by eating their elders and betters. Plot 4 can be used in conjunction with Plots 1, 2, and 3, with the reservation that since the action is set in the far future, there is no longer any need to trouble with mediæval trifles such as rocket-fuels and mass ratio.

Plot No. 5. This is not interplanetary at all, but concerns some other aspect of science. Mutation is a favourite, with time travel also much to the fore. Either human beings are deformed by exposure to radiation, so that they produce hideous monsters instead of children, or else the discovery of a time machine projects the hero and heroine into a future world beside which the scene of Orwell's *1984* would seem like a Victorian drawing-room. I have read one pulp which contained a story describing the feelings of a girl who discovered, rather too late, that her husband was a Martian and that she was about to give birth to a B.E.M. instead of a bouncing baby. The details of what happened later are best left unrecorded, and I hope that no copies of that particular publication are still in existence.

What I have termed the 'Mesozoic' period of science fiction, the Age of Monsters, lasted for a remarkably long time. It reached its heyday about 1934, by which year it had spread from America to Europe. The one saving grace was that the pulps were intended for adult consumption, and were written in a style which made them more or less unintelligible to children (or to anyone else, for that matter).

When war came, in 1939, printing was severely restricted, and the pulps began to die out, leaving only the magazines which had never sunk to such a level. When printing recommenced, about 1946, the whole interplanetary position had changed. German V2 rockets had soared to heights of over a hundred miles, liquid fuels had been developed, and the various Interplanetary Societies had become respected and serious scientific bodies instead of the butts of alleged music-hall comedians. The effect upon science fiction was profound, and there appeared stories which were good literature as well as good science.

But if the adult pulp had had its day, the juvenile pulp had not. This leads us directly to the burning question of the Horror Comic.

A great deal has been heard of these publications. They have been discussed in Parliament and in Congress; exhibitions of them have been held; they have been denounced by teachers, by medical men, and even by politicians. And, unhappily, they have always been linked with science fiction, at least in the popular mind.

This link is only partly real. It cannot be denied that the worst of the pulps are the direct ancestors of juvenile horror comics, but there are also many horror comics which have nothing whatever to do with science. In my view, at least, the most dangerous of all are the 'crime comics,' in which the hero—or criminal, whichever way one looks at it—escapes scot-free throughout all the episodes except possibly the last, when he commits suicide. There are many cases of children who have committed serious offences, even murder, largely because they have been steeped in crime through reading these comics. Anyone who doubts this will do well to read a work called *Seduction of the Innocent,* by Dr Fredric Wertham, in which numerous instances are cited. To deal with these would require a complete book, and would in any case be outside my theme, but it is clear that the trouble cannot be laid wholly at the science writer's door.

I recently obtained several dozens of post-war comics, and it will be informative to outline some of the plots contained in them.

1. *The Temptress of Jupiter.*—Intrepid space-men journey to Jupiter, which proves to be a world of icy cliffs, geysers of molten lava, and seas of ammonia. They then find a lovely and innocent-looking valley, and meet with a beautiful girl, who seems to be able to manage very well without using anything so cumbersome as a space-helmet. One of the explorers is persuaded to take off his helmet so that the girl may kiss him, and then: "a different fate was his than the kiss of a queen's lips! Instantly her body burst into flame! And as Pete's body flamed and withered into ashes in the fatal embrace of fire, the valley of wonder and beauty churned into an inferno!" (Pete's last words were, appropriately enough, "AAAAEEEH! I'm on fire! AAAAGHH!") The surviving explorers take off hastily, and return to Earth. End of the story.

2. *Ulric the Mighty.*—Three Martians have stolen the

secret formula of a new atomic weapon. Ulric the Mighty, who has acquired peculiar powers by living on a diet of radioactive food, is ordered to recover the plans. He chases the Martians to an anonymous asteroid, and kills one of them with his ray-gun; he then strikes the other across the face. "The Martian gave a sudden shriek of agony as Ulric's power coursed through him. His skin turned red and fiery, scorched and burned by the radiant heat, and he fell forward, dead." Ulric recovers the stolen plans and returns home. End of the story.

3. *Catastrophe Dan, the Interplanetary Man.*[1]—This frankly defeats me. It consists of three pages of pictures, the first of which appears to have no conceivable connexion with the other two. It is, however, established that the old professor has discovered the secret of time-travel, and is preparing to send his young assistant, Mark Felton, back through history. Unfortunately he forgets how to get him back, leaving the luckless traveller stranded in the year 1606. Later, it is found that a young man named Mark Felton was burned at the stake for witchcraft in 1606. The inference is obvious. End of the story.

4. *The Specimens.*—Two explorers land on Venus, and bring back with them a single-celled sea-creature. They crash in the ocean on their return home, and the creature escapes. It grows to a tremendous size, and attacks a terrestrial liner. Fortunately it cannot shut its mouth, and is destroyed by the simple expedient of pouring acid into its body until it dies in agony. End of the story.

Apparently the publishers consider that these and other bed-time stories are perfectly suitable reading matter for children aged eight to thirteen. Nor is the distribution confined to juveniles. I remember once travelling from London to East Grinstead in a railway carriage containing six young National Service soldiers. Five of them were reading comics, and the sixth was asleep.

---

[1] A parodied title?

Adults should be able to make up their own minds as to a literary diet, and in any case a horror comic is no more harmful than a thoroughly dirty novel acclaimed by the reviewers and approved by the psychiatrists. But the effect of these comics upon children is a real problem, and one that has yet to be faced, even though some sort of action has been taken.

I must stress that I do not consider all comics to be definitely harmful, and in this respect I am not prepared to go quite as far as Dr Wertham. Some of the comics are absolutely innocuous. Two of Dr Wertham's arguments, however, are difficult to counter, and the more serious of these affects the problems of the English teacher.

The arrangement of the comic strip does not help a child to learn how to read properly. Instead of connected sentences, there are disjointed snatches of conversation written inside balloons, always in capital letters, and without punctuation, apart from the inevitable string of exclamation marks at the end of each section. Dr Wertham places great emphasis upon this, and as a former schoolmaster with over ten years' experience I agree with him whole-heartedly. The comic can be followed without reference to the written material, insofar as it can be said to make sense at all, and a child who has difficulty with reading will merely look at the pictures. Moreover, the printing in the worse comics is such that the words are often semi-illegible.

The words in balloons also lead to the exclamation-mark disease. It appears that the authors in question have never heard of any other kind of punctuation, but what they lack in variety they make up in quantity. A comic in my possession has thirty-one exclamation marks on a single page, six of them occurring together after the word WHAM!!!!!! The vocabulary is decidedly limited, and even worse are the interjections. The following examples come from three comics, all of them published in Great Britain:

"*Screeeeeeeechhhh!*" (as the hero is attacked by a monster bird.)

Bug-Eyed Monsters—and Others 83

"*Erck! Uck! Ick!!*" (Fragment of intergalactic dialogue.)

"*Oooh! Groan!*" (as the hero is hit on the head by a peevish Martian, shown in the act of running away saying "*Heh! heh!*)

"*Owoooorah!*" (The voice of the Tigerthon, a fierce B.E.M. living on the planet Kurl.)

"*Aaaaaaeeeeh! Aaaaaghh!*" (as the hero is decanted bodily into a lake of molten lava.)

"*Yeeeow!*" (as a victim is being throttled in the course of a pleasant little story entitled *The Midnight Horror*.)

Sounds of crashing space-craft, falling men, exploding atom-bombs, and the like are similarly treated. Examples are: "Zeeeee!!" "Woooosh!!" "Crrrrrrump!!!" "Vump!" "Wump!" "Blam!!" "Krack!!!" "Wop!!" "Bop!!" and "Ker-rash!!!!"

This sort of thing does not really make for proper appreciation of the English language, and it occurs, though in modified form, even in comics which are otherwise harmless. In fact, the comic is a perfect pest to the English teacher.

Another objection to all comics is that they are scientifically unsound. This may seem to be a minor matter; after all, many children will live out their lives without paying any attention to science, but it seems a pity to be incorrect when it is so easy to be accurate. I should be inclined to overlook this but for the fact that the life-forms on other worlds are always depicted as being evil. I have no particular objection to a benevolent B.E.M. such as that shown on the jacket to this book, and for reasons given later I do feel that there is a loophole for them in some juvenile books, but we can well dispense with the odd creatures described in stories with graphic titles such as *Planet of Doom, Brute-Men of the Black Planet*, and *Vixens of Venus*.

Quite apart from B.E.M.'s, there are other obvious inaccuracies which could well be weeded out of the harmless comics. There is, for instance, the question of What the Well-Dressed Space-Man Will Wear. The general idea seems to be that one has only to put on a fishbowl helmet, an anti-gravity belt, and a diver's outfit to be able to hop from planet to planet much as a squirrel leaps from tree to tree.

The actual position is very different. To begin with, a pressurized suit will be essential. Water, as we know, boils at sea-level at a temperature of 212 degrees Fahrenheit, but if taken to the top of Mount Everest a kettle would boil at only 186 degrees Fahrenheit, because of the reduced air-pressure. Blood, too, can boil, and at a height of 63,000 feet above sea-level the boiling-point would be reduced to 98·4 degrees Fahrenheit, which is the temperature of the human body. With a diver-type suit, therefore, the space-man would find his blood boiling literally as well as metaphorically, and the consequences would be somewhat uncomfortable. A true space-suit will have to be a perfectly pressurized unit, and will probably be in the form of a metal cylinder, with mechanically operated arms and legs. There is no analogy with the case of the diver. The undersea explorer is concerned mainly with avoiding being squashed by the tremendous pressure, whereas outside the atmosphere there is no pressure at all. (On planets such as Marduk, Voracia, and Plenj, space-clothing can, of course, be discarded entirely.)

Comic-strip interplanetary rockets are always sleek and streamlined, with tapering wings and fins. Their creators forget that streamlining is quite useless in vacuum, and that genuine space-craft of the future are much more likely to be spherical, though at the present moment it is pointless to make many definite forecasts.

All this shows, without the shadow of a doubt, that the horror comic which combines unpleasantness with inaccuracy, and even sex, is a thoroughly bad influence. How can it be combated?

Censorship in any form is repugnant to us, whatever may be the practice in other countries, and this is clearly not the answer. The best solution is for parents and teachers to make sure that undesirable literature is not in evidence, and to point out its shortcomings whenever it appears. In time, it is to be hoped that the offending publishers will realize the harm that they are doing, so that the printing of horror comics will cease.

Yet—and this cannot be too strongly stressed—comics, horror or otherwise, are not representative of science fiction, while the pulp magazines of the twenties and thirties are now practically extinct. To condemn all scientific novels out of hand is narrow-minded and unreasonable, and the sooner we realize it the better.

6

THE MODERN MAGAZINE

During the war years, as we have seen, printing was naturally restricted, with disastrous results to many old-established periodicals. Science fiction did not escape, but strangely enough the results were beneficial. The chief casualties were the pulps, and few if any were issued after 1939.

When conditions became normal once again, the whole interplanetary picture had changed. Consequently the pulps never re-established themselves, and in their place emerged magazines of the modern form, which are at least a vast improvement.

With a few exceptions, the monthly science-fiction periodicals of to-day are harmless. Moreover, they contain a fair proportion of good stories, and B.E.M.'s have faded into the background, though they still reappear now and then. Yet the magazines still fail in some respects; even now they are not properly representative of classical science fiction, mainly because they are technically incorrect. We still meet rockets travelling much faster than light towards planets such as Lor, LaSalle, and Krogan IV; hollow Moons; inhabited asteroids; and hard-bitten, toughened old space veterans forcing their rusty and meteor-pitted ships from Earth to Mars. There is as yet no periodical which concentrates upon Type 2 fiction.

Many of the modern science-fiction periodicals are interplanetary. This is, of course, because space-travel is so much in the public eye at the moment, and in view of the Earth-satellite programme is likely to remain so. Some magazines contain other types of science fiction as well, but even these devote a great deal of attention to the planets.

Just as the B.E.M. was the curse of the pulps, so what I call the Gloom Story is the curse of the modern science-fiction periodical. Innumerable stories end with the hero's soliloquy as he prepares to suffer a fate decidedly worse than death, and beings of other worlds are as evil as they were in the Mesozoic thirties. This kind of thing is all very well provided that it is done skilfully and in moderation, but the magazines contain so much of it that it tends to become monotonous. The Gloom writers pervade the whole field, and even embrace the farthest reaches of the galaxy. Why should beings on planets such as Vega I, Capella II, Rigel III, or even Plenj and Thoss be regarded as essentially evil? We know very little about the universe as a whole, but any such assumption is senseless; if carbon-based life does in fact exist elsewhere, as is extremely probable, it may well be more advanced than our own. The Vegans or Rigelians might even regard Earthmen as bloodthirsty savages, and it would be hard to blame them.

Recently I read through six 1955 monthly science-fiction magazines, containing a total of twenty-nine stories. Of these, twenty-one dealt either with hostile aliens, unpleasant space diseases, or the menace to Earth. It is only fair to add that the remaining eight were original enough to be really interesting, and at least six were cleverly written, but only one made any pretence at technical accuracy.

The 'Menace to Earth' theme is depressingly frequent. It may be due in part to the after-effects of Wells's *War of the Worlds*, probably the most widely-read science-fiction book ever written, but it has been badly overplayed. Only the literary skill of a Wells can save it from disaster.

Another overplayed plot concerns 'space sickness,' coupled with pseudo-medical details which would be better left out. What generally happens is that human mutants are produced as soon as Terrans[1] are unwise enough to pass beyond the shielding atmosphere of their home planet, thus exposing

---

[1] Magazine space-fictionese for 'Earthmen.'

themselves to radiations coming from deep space. And yet a third plot deals with the luckless telepath, who finds himself hated and shunned by his fellow-men much as a professed witch was hated in the days when Kepler wrote his *Somnium*. A headmaster friend of mine recently estimated that of every ten magazine stories, two were worth reading and the rest acted merely as soporifics.

Against all this, it must be stressed once more that the leading science-fiction periodicals are quite harmless, and can be enjoyed by people who prefer stories of such a standard. Moreover, there is always something to be gained from sifting through a pile of such magazines, since good and original stories will be found at fairly regular intervals. In fact, I have no quarrel with the magazines as such; my only criticism is that they tend to bring true scientific literature into disfavour, because of their high percentage of Gloom stories, and because accurate science is almost totally lacking.

One or two of these periodicals have begun to include articles which are meant to be genuinely scientific. Here, again, the standard is very variable. Some of the articles are excellent, whereas others can only be regarded as puerile; the trouble arises from the fact that the non-technical reader has no means of telling which is which. Anyone who learns his astronomy or rocketry solely from magazine articles is certain to end up in a state of mental confusion, whether he realizes it or not.

An example of this will, perhaps, be relevant. The July 1955 issue of one popular science-fiction magazine carried an article in which it was stated categorically that no astronomer has the remotest notion of the speed of light in outer space, and in which Einstein was referred to as the inventor of a curved space which, "according to another aspect of his own distinguished daftness," cannot be curved except relative to something else. I do not for a moment suppose that the author meant the article to be taken seriously, but I do maintain that it could have misled a layman.

I also remember having a letter from a correspondent who pointed out several major mistakes in a book by the then Astronomer Royal, Sir Harold Spencer Jones. The critic was confident of his ground, as he stated that the Astronomer Royal's views were not in accord with the article in the latest monthly periodical. He added, casually, "I suppose Mr Spencer Jones must be out of date." I later found that the critic was aged fourteen and a half.

Another personal experience of mine occurred in 1954. I had been lecturing to the Australian Society of Writers, and at the end of my talk I asked for questions. One member of the audience promptly took me to task for saying that "so far as we know at the moment, the only way to cross space is by rocket." He contended, of course, that atomic power will eventually supersede anything so crude as rocketry. What he failed to realize was that a rocket is still a rocket whether its power is produced by liquid fuels, by atomic motors, or—for that matter—by clockwork. Whatever the fuel, the result is the same; matter is expelled from the exhaust, and the space-craft depends wholly upon the principle of reaction.

Reviews are, of course, often included in science-fiction magazines, and great caution is necessary in reading them. The general problem of reviewing requires, however, a chapter to itself, and can be deferred for the moment.

So far I have spoken entirely about magazines produced in Britain and the U.S.A., and it may be of interest to say something about similar publications in other countries. Sweden, where most people are avid readers of all kinds of literature, is particularly interesting in this respect.

The first Swedish science-fiction magazine appeared in 1939, just after the outbreak of war. It was called *Jules Verne Magasinet*, a name which speaks for itself, though subsequently the publishers changed the title to *Veckans Aventyr*, presumably because they realized that they could not compete with the great French writer, even if they had hoped to do so. (Verne's books have always been popular in

Sweden.) *Veckans Aventyr* died out about 1945, but in 1951 a new periodical appeared under the name of *Häpna*. It still flourishes, and seems to be at least as good as the best British or American science-fiction magazines, though I hesitate to commit myself too definitely, as I cannot read Swedish and have had to depend upon translations. *Häpna's* strong point is that it reprints stories written by the leading science-fiction authors of all countries, and is judicious in its choice. Less than half its contributions are written by Swedish authors.

Very few really bad science-fiction books have appeared in Sweden, and even these are now out of print, so that those who thrive on death-rays and B.E.M.'s have to turn to the cheap and badly written serials that appear in a few weekly papers. It seems that the Swedes prefer 'Type 2' to 'Type 1.' The situation in Norway and Denmark is similar; *Häpna* has a wide circulation throughout Scandinavia.

Other countries have developed their science fiction along similar lines. Germany, for instance, has several good periodicals and very few bad ones. Probably this is due to the fact that the pulps, mainly American and therefore written in 'English,' affected Britain much more seriously than other European countries. Few of them were translated into foreign languages, so that their influence on the Continent has been less disastrous.

So much for the official science-fiction magazines, which are naturally produced purely as commercial ventures. There remain the amateur publications, known as 'fanzines,' which are generally duplicated instead of printed, and which have limited circulations.

Readers of Type 1 science fiction are, above all, clannish. They meet, they talk, they exchange ideas and publications, and now and then a new fanzine is born. What generally happens is that it is launched on the crest of a wave of enthusiasm, survives for a few issues, becomes irregular in appearance, and then dies. The career of a fanzine is not unlike that of a may-bug, which has its period of under-

The Modern Magazine

ground preparation, enjoys its brief hour of glory, and suffers a speedy decease. Each fanzine depends largely upon its editor, partly because he alone is the selector of material, and partly because he usually ends up by writing most of the fanzine himself.

As usual, the standard is variable. I recently read through one fanzine, published in Gateshead, and came to the last page without having gathered the faintest notion of what it was all about. On the other hand, fanzines sometimes discover a new, young, and potentially first-class writer, and for this reason they are always worth looking at. Moreover, they are harmless. There may be offensive fanzines, but I have not encountered them myself.

One trouble facing the fanzine editor is that of production. Printing costs money, and few amateurs have the money to launch a full-scale production, particularly if they are busy with their normal work (or school) all day and every day. Duplication is the obvious alternative, but is seldom really successful. Of a dozen fanzines sent to me recently, four were practically illegible, while the rest included a number of typing mistakes, mis-spellings, and other obvious faults. Yet the standard of literature in at least three of them was remarkably high, and the stories were more original than in the average professional publication.

Though many of the science-fiction magazines to be found on every bookstall are improving their standard each year, we cannot pretend that the position is yet satisfactory. The Gloom School is still too much in evidence, and the death-ray and the menace to Earth have long since become tedious. The obvious remedy is for the establishment of a magazine devoted exclusively to Type 2 fiction, proper scientific articles, and sound reviews. Something of the sort is bound to be launched before very long, and it will deserve to be successful. For the moment we must wait in patience.

I should not like it to be thought that I have anything against the average science-fiction magazine of to-day; all

I am saying is that it is not representative of true science fiction as written by Jules Verne, Godwin, and Lucian. And so long as the Gloom School retains its hold, official prejudice against all science fiction will remain. Some months ago, for instance, I found a magazine left upon the rack of a railway compartment. It proved to be a science-fiction monthly, and I opened it, to be confronted with the sentence: "Somebody cindered Mullard's head with a type 7 blaster." Not unnaturally, I closed the magazine and returned it to the rack, where it probably still remains.

Space-men of the future are, I feel, unlikely to use blasters —type 7 or otherwise.

7

THE NEW OUTLOOK IN SCIENCE FICTION

THE year 1865 was a memorable one in the history of science fiction. It marked the publication of Jules Verne's *From the Earth to the Moon*, one of the most important scientific novels ever written, and which was, in fact, the signal for the opening of a new phase. Almost at the same time appeared Achille Eyraud's *Voyage to Venus*.

Eyraud himself is far from being outstanding from a purely literary point of view. So far as I know, he wrote no other book worthy of mention, and even *Voyage to Venus* is a poor effort considered as a story. Copies of it are now very hard to find, and the text was certainly never translated into English. Moreover, the book suffered under the disadvantage of having been produced at about the same time as Verne's; and even in 1865 Verne was a writer of enormous popularity both inside and outside France.

Yet, ironically enough, Eyraud's basic ideas were much sounder than those of his great contemporary. Whereas Verne clung to the quite impracticable space-gun, and used rockets only to carry his projectile over a completely mythical "neutral point," Eyraud planned to use rocketry for the whole trip. He explained that a firework rises by reaction, and that the recoil of a gun is due to the same cause. He even went so far as to describe a "reaction motor," which is merely an adaptation of the recoil mechanism of a rifle.

The difference between Eyraud's story and the earlier fire-cracker tale of Cyrano is that Eyraud knew quite well what he was doing, whereas Cyrano merely hit upon a correct solution by accident and remained blissfully unaware that he had done so. These happy flukes are not so uncommon as might be imagined, and there are even cases of scientists who have made important discoveries by following some completely wrong theory.

It was not until over thirty years after the publication of Eyraud's book that the Russian scientist Konstantin Eduardovitch Ziolkovsky[1] put forward the reaction-motor idea in a serious article, and even then he was not taken seriously, possibly because Verne's space-gun had taken too firm a hold upon the popular mind. However, Ziolkovsky himself certainly never heard of Eyraud or his book. He was a curious, retiring figure, handicapped by deafness, and his knowledge of the outside world was curiously limited. One famous story about him illustrates this. When a young man of about twenty-five, he submitted some scientific papers to the St Petersburg Society. These papers included a number of formulæ which Ziolkovsky believed to be new, but which had actually been worked out a quarter of a century earlier! This is no reflection upon Ziolkovsky; his formulæ were perfectly sound, but in view of his ignorance of established scientific work, we can appreciate that he can hardly have come across a book by an obscure foreign writer such as Achille Eyraud.

Some years later followed Edward Everett Hale's *The Brick Moon*. J. O. Bailey, in his historical science-fiction work *Pilgrims through Space and Time*, states that this story first appeared in 1870; but I have managed to track it back to its source, and have unearthed it in a periodical called *Atlantic Monthly*, dated October 1869. As a literary effort it can only be described as atrocious, but its ideas are interesting. To make it easier to measure longitude, some young and enterprising scientists decide to provide the Earth with an extra satellite. Accordingly they build a brick moon two hundred feet across, and launch it by a

---

[1] Some writers spell this name 'Tsiolkovskii.' Since the Russians do not use our alphabet, the sensible method seems, however, to be phonetic, and in my view 'Tsiolkovskii' is about as logical as spelling the word zebra 'tsebraa.'

The New Outlook in Science Fiction

weird and wonderful arrangement of flywheels. Unfortunately a slight mishap results in its being sent nine thousand miles out into space, carrying thirty-seven people with it. Since the miniature world has been thoughtful enough to take its own atmosphere with it, the members of the crew are not particularly worried; food is sent up to them by the same flywheel mechanism, and they signal to their earth-bound friends by jumping up and down in the Morse code. Despite its many shortcomings, there can be little doubt that Hale's brick moon is the first artificial satellite in history.

The next science-fiction work of any note was Percival Greg's *Across the Zodiac*, published in 1880. Here we have an anti-gravity device in the shape of a counter-electric force, apergy, which suffices to send an Earthman to Mars. The atmosphere of the Red Planet is, of course, breathable, and the bold adventurer finds an advanced civilization. During his stay on the planet he manages to acquire half a dozen wives, in accordance with normal Martian custom, but eventually decides to return to the comparative peace of his own world. Perhaps he was wise.

André Laurie, in his *Conquest of the Moon* (1889), approached the interplanetary problem in a different manner. Following the principle of Mahomet and the mountain, he decided that if he could not go to the Moon he would bring the Moon down to the Earth. In his tale a group of financiers make up their minds to exploit the mineral resources of the lunar crust, and after rejecting the idea of building a tube from one world to the other they hit upon a more ingenious ruse. They insulate a large iron-ore mountain in the Sahara Desert by fusing the sand round it, and then magnetize the mountain by means of generators fed by batteries of sun-mirrors. The Moon is brought closer and closer to the Earth, but at last one member of the party panics and reverses the switch. Immediately the mountain, the observatory, and the crew are plucked from the ground and swept upward until they land in a lunar valley. Their return is made by parachute, a method practicable owing to the fact that the Moon is still only just beyond the limits of the Earth's atmosphere. Oddly enough, nobody will believe their story.[1]

Books such as *Across the Zodiac* and *Conquest of the Moon* were entertaining and pleasant, though less scientific than Verne's and Eyraud's. But in 1897 came the famous *Auf Zwei Planeten* (*On Two Planets*), by Kurd Laszwitz,[2] Professor of Mathematics at Gotha, which returns to something much more substantial. Again the method of space-travel is incorrect, but the story contains a remarkable amount of accurate material. Laszwitz was, indeed, well equipped to write a sound scientific novel. He was a competent mathematician, astronomer, and natural historian, and he had sat in the Prussian Landtag, so that he was thoroughly used to debate and argument. Moreover, he shared Verne's gift of being able to control his imagination. It is a great pity that *Auf Zwei Planeten* has never been translated into English; such a translation would be welcomed even now. The latest German edition was published as recently as 1948.

In Laszwitz's book the secret of space-travel is discovered not by Earthmen, but by the Martians, an older and more advanced race than our own. (The horrific Martians of later days had yet to make their entrance.) Their method was to build a complete shell of anti-gravity material. So long as the shell remained open it was subject to gravity in the normal way; but as soon as it was complete its weight vanished, so that it drifted off into an orbit of its own. What the Martians did, therefore, was to complete the shell and wait until their own planet had been obliging enough to remove itself from underneath them. They then fell towards the Sun until they reached the orbit of the Earth, and landed without difficulty.

The closed-shell idea was an improvement upon Wells's cavorite, which became weightless as soon as it had cooled

---

[1] It is rather surprising to find that Bailey mentions neither Laurie's book nor Eyraud's.
[2] Alternatively spelled "Lasswitz."

The New Outlook in Science Fiction

to a certain temperature. The whole principle is, of course, unworkable, but the interesting point is that Laszwitz had more or less hit upon the principle of 'free fall' which has become of such enormous importance in modern studies. To make this clearer, let us pause to consider the actual position.

The Earth moves at a speed of approximately $18\frac{1}{2}$ miles a second. This is not an arbitrary speed; it is the only possible one for a body travelling round the Sun at a distance of 93 million miles. Nor is it quite constant, since the Earth moves fastest when at its minimum distance from the solar surface—bearing in mind, of course, that its orbit is not perfectly circular.

Kepler, author of the *Somnium*, demonstrated this mathematically in his Second Law. This Law states that the radius vector of a planet—*i.e.*, the imaginary line joining the centre of the planet to the centre of the Sun—moves over equal

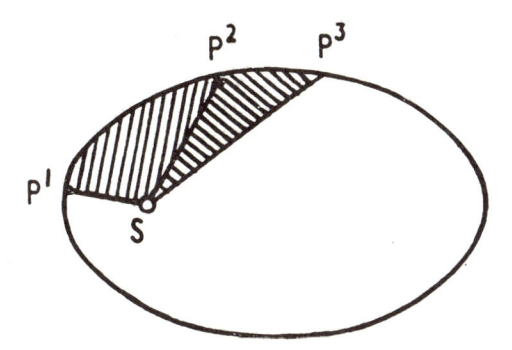

areas in equal times. In the diagram, S is the Sun and P¹, P², and P³ a planet at different positions in its orbit.[1] If the time taken to move from P¹ to P² is the same as that taken to move from P² to P³, then the triangle P¹SP² must be equal in area to the triangle P²SP³. In other words,

[1] For the sake of clarity the eccentricity of the orbit of planet P has been made much greater than that of any actual planet.

Planet P moves quickest when near the Sun, slowing down when it becomes more remote.

It follows that the closest planets to the Sun are the greyhounds of the Solar System. Mercury (average distance 36 million miles) hurries along at 30 miles a second; Venus (67 million miles) at 21¾. Mars (141 million miles) is a comparative sluggard, ambling in its path at a mere 15 miles a second.

Suppose that the Earth could speed up? Immediately its orbit would change; it would start to move outward, slowing gradually down in the absence of any further impetus. Finally the orbit would become an ellipse of greater eccentricity. There is no known force which can alter the Earth's speed, unless we are prepared to drag in an improbable accident such as the intrusion of a wandering star, but the principle can be used for a space-ship which is capable of being speeded up by means of rockets.

Once beyond the atmosphere, and thus able to move at any speed without being burned up like a meteor by friction against air-particles, the ship will be accelerated. Instead of moving along in company with the Earth, it will draw outward until it reaches Mars. If all the calculations are correct and no careless professor has confused a full-stop with a decimal point, ship and Mars will then meet, and a landing can be effected. Of course, the practical difficulties are immense; but it can be seen that once the first impetus has been given, there will be no need to go on using up fuel in order to apply more power. When the ship has entered its new orbit, it will swing outward on its own. It will, in fact, have entered a free orbit. On the return journey the procedure can be applied in reverse. The ship will be slowed down instead of speeded up, and it will swing inward towards the Sun.

Laszwitz appreciated this, and was undoubtedly the first to do so in the proper sense of the word. He did not fall into the still-common trap of making his space-craft plunge straight across the void direct from Earth to Mars. The shortest route is, in fact, an uneconomical one, and will never be used until we have learned how to draw upon almost unlimited supplies of power.

This is obvious enough. Swinging outward in free orbit, we can let matters take their course. If the initial thrust is right and the timing is right we shall reach Mars, provided that minor corrections are made by using rocket power in limited bursts—a point that Laszwitz did not overlook. If, however, we plan to move straight outward from the Sun we shall have to go on applying power all the time, and this is out of the question because of the amount of fuel necessary.

According to Laszwitz, the first Martian attempts at space-travel were disastrous, partly because of the clumsiness of the method and partly because the gravity-shielding matter disintegrated when it entered the humid atmosphere of the Earth. As they experimented, however, the Martians learned how to erect a space-station above the Earth's pole, and subsequently built a base at the Pole itself, where it was discovered by a party of terrestrial balloonists.

The description of the Martians themselves is also of interest. Though wiser and more advanced than Earthmen, they yet retained many human weaknesses. The canals of Mars were said to be vegetation strips across the ochre deserts, each being cultivated round a stream of piped water, so that the whole planet could be made habitable by a system of irrigation. This may sound fantastic in 1956; it was certainly not fantastic in 1897, when the canals were widely regarded as artificial. Only a decade later Professor Percival Lowell put forward the same idea in his strictly scientific book *Mars and its Canals*.

Laszwitz's book made quite a stir. It was translated into almost every European language except English, and it led to the reissue of Kepler's *Somnium*, while it may also have influenced H. G. Wells when he created cavorite. Oddly enough, however, it remained more or less in a class by itself. Other writers preferred to follow Wells or Verne, and anti-gravity and the space-gun retained their hold. A modified gravity device was used, for instance, in George Griffith's *Honeymoon in Space*, published in 1901, in which the happy couple visit Mars, Venus, Jupiter, and Saturn, apparently finding breathable atmospheres everywhere—even though the Saturnian air did prove to be a soupy substance in which swam jellyfish the size of whales.

The great scientific advances of the twenties, due in large measure to the work of Oberth and Goddard, did not produce the desired effect. They led instead to the rise of B.E.M.'s horror stories, and the pulps. Why this should have been so has always remained a mystery to me, but once the pulps had become prominent, most reputable writers began to shun science fiction altogether. (There were, of course, one or two exceptional books, such as R. C. Sherriff's *The Hopkins Manuscript*.)

The death of the pulps marked the beginning of another swing of the pendulum. When the revival came, in or about 1946, it took a new form. Leading authors set out to combine imagination with accuracy, and—mercifully—the modern school of science fiction came into being.

The new trend meant, of course, that the serious science-fiction writer had to learn up his facts. Some authors were apparently incapable of doing so, and turned back to cowboys and Indians, while others evaded the issue either by concentrating upon stories set in the far future or the remote past, or by creating grizzled, hard-boiled space veterans whose sole mission in life was to uncover dope-rings led by unscrupulous Martians, though they remained sufficiently human to acquire numerous beautiful and ray-gun-toting damsels in the process.

But for true science fiction, an authentic background had become essential. Consider the analogy of the historical novel, a very old and respected branch of literature. A story which centres round Napoleon's victory at Waterloo is not likely to be well received, simply because practically every one knows that Napoleon did not win at Waterloo. Obvious historical mistakes will ruin even a well-written story. Similarly, most people know by now that B.E.M.'s, anti-gravity, and space-guns are equally out of the question, and novels which make use of them cannot be taken seriously except by those who do not trouble to think. Type 1 stories may, of course, be entertaining and amusing; but, like the monthly magazines, they must not be confused with proper scientific fiction.

One of the leaders of the new school was—and is—Arthur C. Clarke, former chairman of the British Interplanetary Society. In *The Sands of Mars*, generally (and, in my view, rightly) regarded as an outstanding science-fiction novel of the post-war period, Clarke paints a good picture of what a Martian trip will probably be like, coupled with a perfectly sound description of the Red Planet itself. There is a strong plot, and enough imaginative material is introduced to satisfy the most carping critic, but the fact remains that his book is technically correct. In *Prelude to Space* he describes the preparations leading up to the departure of the first lunar ship, and in *Earthlight* the action takes place entirely on the Moon.

It is easy to see the importance of this method. There are many people who will never force themselves to read a technical book, even a popular one such as Jeans' *The Universe around Us* or, for that matter, Clarke's own *Exploration of Space*. They will, however, devour a well-written novel. If they learn something in the process, so much the better, and Type 2 fiction can play a major rôle in the suppression of wrong ideas. On the other hand, it is still necessary to be cautious. In a novel published in 1954 we meet with an earth satellite flying round the Earth at a height of forty miles, whereas in point of fact such a satellite would be destroyed very quickly owing to the heat set up by friction.

Actually, investigation of the air-density at high altitudes is one of the main reasons for launching the new Earth satellites. It would be wrong to regard them as space-ships, or even the ancestors of true space-ships; they are mainly designed to investigate the upper atmosphere. It is planned to launch them in 1957 or 1958, and there is no reason to suppose that there will be any major delays in the general programme.

The popular nickname of 'flying footballs' is quite apt. The first satellites will be tiny bodies two or three feet in diameter, and it is possible that the preliminary launchings will be of 'footballs' that do not even carry instruments. They will be set in orbits from 200 to 300 miles above the Earth, and this means that they will complete one circuit of the globe in about ninety minutes. They will not, however, remain up indefinitely. Even at this height there is still appreciable atmosphere, and this atmosphere will set up friction, which will gradually slow the 'footballs' down. They will spiral gradually towards the ground, until they enter the denser air, when they will suffer the same fate as meteors: they will be heated to incandescence, will burst into flame, and will be destroyed. How long it will take them to enter the danger-zone must remain uncertain for the moment, since our knowledge of the upper air is still very incomplete.

These first attempts will be followed by satellites still of small size, but carrying instruments. The satellites themselves will never be recovered, but while they are in orbit they will be able to send information back to the ground, and they will pave the way for satellites to be set in more distant orbits, far enough from the resisting atmosphere to be safe from being dragged downward. In time these will in their turn be followed by larger and more complex satellites; but that is looking far into the future.

The writing of Type 2 fiction calls for far greater skill than is needed for 'space opera.' One of the obvious difficulties is that of explaining technical terms. A layman who opens a novel to find himself confronted with expressions such as 'longitudinal libration' and 'exaggerated mass-ratio' will probably close the book with a weary sigh and turn back to the usual strong, silent men dodging tomahawks in the Wild West. It is not easy to introduce scientific terms without the reader's realizing that he is being educated, and not many writers have done it successfully, particularly when a strong plot has to be kept going at the same time.

Sex is even more awkward to handle. Once the Venusian vamps and Saturnian sirens have retired baffled, the hapless author is in a quandary. The problem is too important to evade, but I still await a novel with an intriguing title such as *Passion on Pluto* or *He Wooed Her under Zero Gravity*.

It is also a pity that there are so few available planets. Venus offers plenty of scope, since it is still uncertain whether the Planet of Love is a howling dust-desert or a carbon-fouled ocean, but nothing can make it an attractive world. The obvious alternative is to go farther afield to planets of other Solar Systems, but here we run into the interstellar travel difficulty. Transferring a story to the indefinite future is one answer, but we revert immediately to Type 1 fiction, and the authentic background is lost.

However, the main trouble about scientifically sound literature is that there is so little of it. There are unlimited opportunities here for anyone who is prepared to tackle the subject seriously, but so far at least very few writers have cared to do so. Only when the need for accuracy is fully realized will science fiction regain the status it enjoyed before the Period of the Pulps.

8

JUVENILE SCIENCE FICTION

APART from the horror comics and their regrettable camp-followers, we have so far dealt only with adult science fiction. There is, of course, an equally wide range in the juvenile field, but the problems of boys' science fiction are not always realized.

A few crusty folk stubbornly refuse to admit that adult science fiction exists at all, and dismiss books, short stories, and comics alike as 'kid's stuff.' Before the interplanetary project became a real possibility there may have been a certain amount of justification for this view. It is true that Verne wrote ostensibly for young people, though actually his books are just as fascinating to a stripling of eighty. On the other hand, nobody could call *Across the Zodiac* a child's tale, and even before the turn of the century there were many novels suitable only for adults. Now that the rockets have begun to fly, scientific literature is beginning to take its rightful place. The distinction between juvenile and adult has become much more marked since the end of the War.

Even in the Mesozoic thirties some good boys' stories were published in magazines and annuals. I well remember a series by Murray Roberts, which ran through a now-defunct and lamented paper called *The Modern Boy*. Here we had all the ingredients to be expected: the white-haired, absent-minded old Professor Flaznagel; the dauntless Captain Justice; the jovial Irish doctor, and the inevitable red-haired scamp, Midge. Several of Roberts' stories were inter-planetary, and most of the rest had a strong scientific basis. I was an avid reader of *The Modern Boy*, and I regret its demise, mainly because it was thoroughly wholesome.

Juvenile Science Fiction

Less worthy were some juvenile magazines which included science fiction, but which were not 'comics' in the true sense of the word. However, these too became war casualties, and we have to admit that nowadays there is a dearth of really good magazines for the boy aged from ten to sixteen, such as the *Boy's Own Paper*.

As with adult literature, we can divide juveniles into Types 1 and 2, the inaccurate and the factual. Here, however, the difficulties of the would-be Type 2 author are more than doubled. Sex cannot be introduced; nor can too much pure science, and nor can profound moral or philosophical considerations. Yet there must be a thrilling story, with action from first to last page if the reader is not to become bored and discard the book in favour of a Western. It is not easy.

Very few purely accurate novels have been produced for the boy reader. Even Arthur Clarke's *Islands in the Sky*, where the action takes place almost entirely out in space, is set some years in the future, at a time when the artificial satellite is already in existence. However, all details are as correct as they can be made at the moment, and the plot certainly does not suffer because of this.

On the other hand, Type 1 stories are almost embarrassingly common. A reviewer in the *Manchester Guardian* recently commented that he had made seven visits to Mars in the course of a single year. It must, however, be stressed that some of the Type 1 juveniles are excellent; no parent or headmaster can possibly object to the stories written by such authors as William F. Temple, Captain W. E. Johns, Angus MacVicar, and Mary Elwyn Patchett.

Temple, for instance, has created "Martin Magnus," a space-hero in every sense of the word. An astronomer might well question some of the discoveries made by Magnus on Venus and the Moon, but few boys are likely to do so. Captain Johns, famous as the writer of the "Biggles" books, has produced two interplanetary stories of similar type, while MacVicar, in *The Lost Planet* and its sequels, describes the adventures of Dr MacKinnon and his crew upon the strange planet Hesikos. Mary Patchett's *Kidnappers of Space* and *Lost on Venus* are other examples. All these authors succeed because their books are skilfully written, exciting, and thoroughly wholesome.

Educating a child is all very well, but there are plenty of suitable books available, and boys have no wish to be instructed all the time. After all, St George's dragon is an excellent example of a B.E.M. And if we can have witches and goblins on Earth, why not on Mars?

The essential point to remember is that dragons, witches, and goblins occur only in juvenile literature. Except in special circumstances, they would be ridiculous in adult novels, and the same argument can be applied to junior science fiction.

In view of what has already been said about comics and inaccurate novels, it may appear dangerous for me to enter a plea for the modified juvenile B.E.M., and I am well aware of the danger. I hold no brief for the slime-covered Venusian or the man-eating hydra from Neptune. I do feel that a certain amount of licence is permissible, but one or two conditions must always be borne in mind.

First, all B.E.M.'s in juvenile literature should be of the comparatively mild variety. A Martian creature should be of the type which might, if we stretch a good many points, flourish there; it should, for instance, have lungs adapted to breathe the thin and oxygen-poor air. Even though no such being can in fact exist, it may be made to sound reasonably plausible, whereas a ten-foot green beast with several heads is 'kid's stuff' and nothing more. It is not even interesting.

Secondly, anything in the nature of unwholesomeness should be avoided at all costs. It also seems a mistake that interplanetary beings are so often ferocious and disgusting in their habits. Why should they be?

And, thirdly, the author should make the nature of his book quite clear. If it is meant to be accurate, and thus in a sense educational, all well and good; if the science is incorrect, the reader should be told so. It will not detract from a boy's enjoyment, and it will mean that there is no danger of giving out false information.

A rather depressing experience of my own may be of interest here. I have written eight or nine boys' science-fiction novels, and in my early days as a writer I produced several full-blooded B.E.M.'s. Some of them fulfilled the second of the conditions given above, but they were B.E.M.'s none the less. Subsequently I made a close study of the science-fiction field, and saw the error of my ways, so that my more recent novels have been—I hope—less fantastic. Not long ago I talked to a boy of thirteen, and gave him one of my early books and also a later one, *Wheel in Space*, which is in accordance with accepted theory. He read them, and made the profound comment: "I think I liked the first one best, because I found the monsters exciting!"

I found it difficult to make an adequate reply.

9

FACT OR FICTION?

ALTHOUGH books in general can be divided into two classes, fact and fiction, it is not always easy to tell which is which. Several allegedly 'scientific' contributions of past years have turned out to be anything but factual, and can thus be included under the broad heading of science fiction. Some were written with the set intention of fooling the public; others were perfectly honest, but had similar results.

Let us begin with a pure hoax. It took place in 1835, over a hundred years ago, and it was remarkably successful. Moreover, it was completely good-humoured, and even Sir John Herschel, the chief victim, is said to have burst out laughing when he first heard what had been going on.

Herschel was one of the most famous astronomers of his day. He was the son of an even more famous father, Sir William Herschel, who had discovered the planet Uranus and had been appointed Court Astronomer to King George III. Sir John inherited much of his father's energy and enthusiasm, and one of his ambitions was to complete the survey of the sky that Sir William had begun. The elder Herschel had spent most of his life in England, and had thus been unable to study the stars of the extreme south, such as the Southern Cross and the Clouds of Magellan, which never rise in our latitudes. Sir John therefore decided to go to the Cape of Good Hope, taking with him a large and powerful telescope.

He reached the Cape without mishap, set up his telescope, and began work. He remained in Africa for several years,

Fact or Fiction?

and by the time he left for home he had accumulated a mass of observations that took more than a decade to sort through and publish. Needless to say, he was concerned only with the stellar heavens. The Moon and planets can be seen from Britain, so that there is no need to cross half the world to observe them. Nevertheless, reports of alleged lunar observations soon began to attract much popular attention. Some sensational articles in a New York paper, the *Sun*, described not only close-up views of the Moon's surface, but even the discovery of weird life-forms there.

The author of these articles was a reporter named Richard Adams Locke. Locke was an Englishman who had emigrated to the United States to take up journalism, and there is no doubt that he combined fertile imagination with unusual opportunism. His reasoning was perfectly sound. Herschel was on the other side of the world; communications in those days were slow and uncertain; who was there to issue a prompt denial of anything that might be printed?

On August 25, 1835, therefore, the *Sun* came out with a headline: "Great Astronomical Discoveries Lately Made by Sir John Herschel, LL.D. F.R.S., &c., at the Cape of Good Hope." The first paragraph is worth quoting in full:

> In this unusual addition to our Journal, we have the happiness of making known to the British public, and thence to the whole civilized world, recent discoveries in Astronomy which will build an imperishable monument to the age in which we live, and confer upon the present generation of the human race proud distinction through all future time. It has been poetically said that the stars of heaven are the hereditary regalia of man as the intellectual sovereign of the animal creation. He may now fold the Zodiac around him with a loftier consciousness of his mental supremacy.

Locke's tongue must have been very much in his cheek, particularly as he went on to describe the new telescope supposed to have been invented by Herschel for his new observations. Locke knew, of course, that the chief limitation of any telescope lies in the fact that it cannot collect enough light for extreme magnification. The biggest telescope ever made up to then was Sir William Herschel's giant forty-eight inch, but even this could not collect enough light to give the observer a really close view of the Moon or any other astronomical body—and in any case it had been dismantled long before 1835. Locke worked round this problem by effecting "a transfusion of artificial light through the focal object of vision." In other words, you use your mirror to form an image, and then brighten the image by reinforcing it from a light-source in the observatory itself, so that almost any magnification can be obtained! Not content with this, Locke told how Herschel had constructed a reflector with a mirror 288 inches in diameter. Even the equally mythical instrument of the Baltimore Gun Club pales by comparison.

The article was so cleverly worded that it sounded almost plausible, and Locke did not make the mistake of over-reaching himself. His next article, published on August 26, was deliberately dry and technical, so that the illusion was well maintained. But in the same issue of the *Sun* appeared an article said to be a direct quotation from an Edinburgh journal, describing not only the mounting of the wonderful telescope, but also Herschel's feelings as he gazed through the eyepiece at the lunar landscape:

> The whole immense power of the telescope was applied, and to its focal image about one half the power of the microscope. On removing the screen of the latter, the field of view was covered throughout its entire area with a beautifully distinct and even vivid representation of basaltic rock. Its colour was a greenish brown; and the width of the columns, as defined by their interstices on the canvas, was invariably 28 inches. . . . This precipitous cliff was profusely covered with a dark red flower.

The *Sun* kept up the good work for the next five days, telling its gasping readers about the further investigations

Fact or Fiction?

of Herschel's team at the Cape. Life forms were next introduced, beginning with "brown quadrupeds having all the external characteristics of the bison, but more diminutive than any species of the bos genus in our natural history," and "a strange amphibious creature, of a spherical form, rolling with great velocity along a pebbly beach." Another interesting creature was

> of a bluish lead colour, about the size of a goat, with a head and beard like him, and a single horn, slightly inclined from the perpendicular. The female was destitute of the horn and beard, but had a much longer tail.... It was gregarious, and chiefly abounded on the acclivitous glades of the woods.... This beautiful creature afforded us the most exquisite enjoyment.

The climax was reached on August 28, with Locke's priceless account of lunar bat-men:

> Certainly they were like human beings.... They averaged four feet in height, were covered, except on the face, with short glossy copper-coloured hair, and had wings composed of a thin membrane, without hair, lying snugly upon their backs, from the top of the shoulders to the calves of the legs. The face, which was of a yellowish flesh colour, was a slight improvement upon that of the large orang-outang, being much more open and intelligent in its expression, and having a much greater expansion of forehead. The mouth, however, was very prominent, though somewhat relieved by a thick beard upon the lower jaw....

Locke was clever enough to force his readers back to 'science' every now and then. Sometimes a higher-powered eyepiece had to be used, sometimes conditions were unsuitable for observations at all, and sometimes it was necessary to turn up the hydro-oxygen burners to light up the faint image by the method of 'artificial transfusion.' The series was brought to an end by an account of how the astronomers forgot to cover up the main mirror, so that when the Sun shone on it it acted as a vast burning-glass and set light to the equipment, causing all work to be abandoned for the time being.

To us this may sound far-fetched, though not more so than the very modern reports of beings in flying saucers, but in 1835 the possibility of lunar life was still under consideration. Sir William Herschel, Sir John's father, had regarded the habitability of the Moon as "an absolute certainty," and went so far as to believe that there were men living inside the Sun; similar views were held by mid-nineteenth-century astronomers, particularly Gruithuisen of Munich. The hostile nature of the Moon was by no means fully appreciated.

The series met with a mixed reception. Some critics swallowed the bait completely, and the *New York Times* wrote that the discoveries were "both possible and probable," adding that Herschel's work had ushered in a new age of scientific development. A women's club in Massachusetts is reported to have written to Herschel asking him his opinion of the best way to get in touch with the bat-men and convert them to Christianity, while several people claimed to have seen the great 288-inch mirror being loaded on to the ship that was to take it to Africa. On the other hand, certain of the universities and academies had their doubts. Yale University sent two well-known astronomers to New York to investigate, and the whole business was debated by the French Académie des Sciences.

The hoax was exposed by a rival New York paper within a few weeks, and the *Sun* itself confessed on September 16. Even then, however, lingering doubts remained, and not for some months was it established once and for all that the 288-inch reflector, the flower-coated lunar cliffs, and the bat-men were pure fiction and nothing else. Henceforth the Moon remained uninhabited until flying saucers started landing there during our own century.

Considered as fiction, Locke's series was a remarkably good effort. It was reprinted in booklet form, and the whole hoax was published anew in 1937 in the periodical *Sky* (now *Sky and Telescope*). It has, of course, served as the basis for several stories. One, R. H. Romans' *The Moon Conquerors*, appeared in the Winter 1930 issue of *Science Wonder Quarterly*, an early American magazine of science fiction which maintained an unusually high standard. Romans, too, described a giant reflector which showed the lunar surface so closely that the activities of the local inhabitants could be followed, and he destroyed the telescope in the same way that Locke had done. The subsequent journey to the Moon was well done, even though the space-ship itself would hardly have met with the approval of Professor Oberth, and the plot was skilfully worked out. B.E.M.'s were conspicuous only by their absence. That particular issue of *Science Wonder Quarterly* also included a good time-travel story and an amusing though fantastic tale about the Earth's interior. I have often wondered why the magazine failed to survive in its original form.

One more obvious hoax should be mentioned, though it took the form of a single article only. One of the most eminent astronomers of the late nineteenth century was Professor Edward Emerson Barnard, who had earned a wide reputation for discovering comets. Barnard was therefore astounded to read a long article in the *San Francisco Examiner* stating that he had invented a "seeker" that would take most of the work off his shoulders, as it would sweep automatically across the heavens and ring a bell as soon as it found a comet. The author of the article was clearly an astronomer, and the description of the wonderful comet-seeker deceived not only laymen, but also a good many scientists. Not unnaturally, Barnard sat down and wrote a frantic disclaimer, only to find that neither the *Examiner* nor any other paper would publish it; they had been 'got at' well in advance. For many months Barnard received congratulations from his scientific colleagues, coupled with requests for further details about his remarkable instrument.

Dr James Price's *Account of Some Experiments with Mercury*,

Silver and Gold, published in July 1782, is different in nature. Nobody knows whether Price was a hoaxer or not, and the mystery is likely to remain unsolved. He was not an astronomer; he was, in fact, an alchemist, and, if he is to be believed, the only successful one in history.

Alchemy is a favourite theme of the fiction-writer, ancient or modern. In brief, it is the art of making gold out of less valuable materials, and is thus a method of getting something for nothing, nowadays beyond the power of anybody but the Chancellor of the Exchequer. Alchemical stories have been written in their hundreds. Sometimes silver is made out of lead; diamonds are produced by heating sawdust, and even radium has been formed by the fusion of common elements such as copper and tin. The Philosopher's Stone and the secret of eternal youth come into the same category.

Until a few centuries ago, alchemy—together with its even more absurd companion, astrology—was regarded as a true science. It can, in fact, be regarded as the ancestor of chemistry, and even though the experimenters failed to produce gold or to find the elixir of life, they did at least make some important chemical advances. Sir Isaac Newton was a convinced alchemist, and even while working at his immortal *Principia* he used to lay down his pen and spend whole nights in his laboratory, working away in his vain quest for the key that would unlock the secrets of the universe.

Dr Price[1] was elected to a Fellowship of the Royal Society at the early age of thirty, and seemed destined for a brilliant career. In his book, however, he claimed that he could make gold by heating a mixture of mercury and a secret 'red powder,' hitherto unknown to science. He added that the experiment had been carried out in the presence of seven unbiased witnesses. The claim led to consternation in the ranks of the Royal Society, and news of it spread all over

---

[1] He was born James Higginbotham, but changed his name by deed poll.

Fact or Fiction?

Europe. It could not be ignored, and Price was asked to repeat the experiment before three referees appointed by the Society.

He delayed as long as he could, but finally agreed, and the referees went down to visit him at his house in Guildford. The sequel was as lurid as anything in a Victorian melodrama. Price went to his laboratory to make the final preparations, and was found there dead, having apparently swallowed poison.

Unless Price had really stumbled upon some vital truth, we must dismiss his book as an elaborate hoax. It is, however, difficult to see what he could have expected to gain; he must have known that he would lose his reputation if he failed to substantiate his claim to make gold, and as things turned out he lost his life as well.

One of the early alchemical stories was Edgar Allan Poe's *Von Kempelen and his Discovery*, published in 1848. Here we have the successful alchemist who is accused of being a forger, and prudently disappears. Something of the same sort came from the pen of H. G. Wells half a century later, in *The Diamond Maker*. Like *Von Kempelen*, it is a short story, and describes how an alchemist offers to sell one of his home-made diamonds for a hundred pounds. The narrator is dubious, but before he can follow up the investigation the diamond-maker is accused of being an anarchist, and decamps.

Jules Verne, in *Star of the South* (1884), dealt with alchemy just as he might have been expected to do. The scientist of the story produces a diamond indeed, but it proves to be an ordinary one, placed in his crucible by a thoughtful servant who did not want his master to be disappointed. *Star of the South* is a full-length novel, and Verne describes the African mines so well that it is hard to realize that he never actually went there.

One of the cleverest alchemical stories of fairly recent times is George Allan England's *The Golden Blight*, first published in 1916. John Storm, the scientist, discovers not the means of making gold, but a Zeta-Ray that will cause existing gold to crumble into ash. He reasons that since money is the root of all evil, the loss of the world's gold reserves will be beneficial, so he wanders about Europe and America destroying all gold within striking distance. Braunschweig, a German financier, is clever enough to realize that the effect of the Zeta-Ray will wear off in time, so he collects the ash and hoards it. It does indeed change back into gold, in the presence of Braunschweig and his colleagues, but in so doing it generates so much heat that the hapless financiers are boiled like potatoes. By this time the people of the world are so disillusioned that they reorganize the whole structure of society, and do not even bother to collect the gold, which is left where Braunschweig had piled it.

Another branch of alchemy concerns the search for 'the secret of life,' and here we find a man whose career has some points in common with that of Price: Andrew Crosse, a shy, retiring man who spent most of his life in his quiet country house in the Quantock Hills. He was interested in science, particularly in electricity, but he had no training worthy of mention, and was what we should now call a dabbler. However, one of his dabbles earned him a notoriety that he could well have done without. For a few months in 1837 he was probably the most hated and feared man in England, simply because he had claimed to be able to produce living creatures from inert matter.

Crosse's method was to allow a weak and long-continued electric current to flow through a certain chemical solution. According to him, this resulted in the appearance of small insects called acari, which seemed to be no different from acari born of normal parents. As with Price, it is not easy to see what he could have been expected to gain from attempting a hoax, and as soon as he met with severe criticism he discontinued his experiments and refused to say any more. The best account of the whole affair is contained in *Memorials, Scientific and Literary*, by C. H. A. Crosse (Andrew's wife), published in 1857, while Commander Rupert Gould—the

Fact or Fiction? 117

"Star-Gazer" of the B.B.C. Children's Hour—summed it up in his fascinating book *Oddities*. A shorter but perfectly accurate account is given in the late Cedric Allingham's *Flying Saucer from Mars*, to which further reference will be made later.

Fortunately, perhaps, nobody else has hit upon the secret, and since Crosse seems to have been a perfectly sincere man, it is probable that he deceived himself as well as others. So far as we know, there is no method of 'making' life. We can make an exact chemical replica of a living entity, indistinguishable by means of normal analysis, but we cannot make it live.

On the other hand, it would be dangerous to say that life creation is absolutely impossible, and the fictional possibilities are immense. The best life-creation novel is, in my view, William F. Temple's *Four-sided Triangle*, published a few years ago. In this tale a young scientist discovers how to produce exact copies of objects which already exist. Duplicating Old Masters is all very well, but when the 'reproducer' turns out a human being there are violent repercussions. The plot is most ingenious, and since the book is also convincingly written, it is calculated to hold the interest from beginning to end.

Otherwise, however, the theme of life creation has become largely the property of the Gloom School, and this applies with equal force to immortality. Dean Swift, in *Gulliver's Voyage to Laputa*, painted a depressing picture of old folk who had all the afflictions of senility and yet could not die, while there have been many lesser stories based on the same idea. (Actually, the genuine longevity record appears to be held by a Norwegian sailor, C. J. Drakenberg, who reached the advanced age of a hundred and forty-eight.[1])

---

[1] The evidence in favour of Drakenberg's age is not conclusive, but it is undeniably strong. A few more cases of extended life are on record. The Countess of Desmond, who lived in the late Stuart times, was certainly at least a hundred and twenty when she died, and was moreover active to the last.

Lastly, some mention must be made of the recent Flying Saucer books. Here I am treading on very thin ice, as the idea of treating such books as fiction will cause raised eyebrows in many quarters. I must make it quite clear that I accuse no one of bad faith, and I am certain that most of the writers concerned are utterly sincere. However, we must face the facts.

U.F.O.'s, or Unidentified Flying Objects, have been reported now and then all through history. Charles Fort, an eccentric American who died twenty years ago, spent a great deal of time collecting accounts of them, and produced four large books dealing with these and other oddities. The books are written in a style which makes them difficult to read and almost impossible to interpret, but they are undeniably fascinating, and it may be that Fort was the first to suggest that the U.F.O.'s are cruising space-craft from another world.

Then, in 1947, came the first reported sightings of U.F.O.'s which were said to be not birds, bats, ice crystals, or auroræ, but flying machines of a hitherto unknown type. The logical development was a report of an actual meeting with a space-man, and before long a Mr Truman Bethurum announced that he had paid several visits to a Saucer which came from the planet Clarion, and was captained by a beautiful woman named Mrs Aura Rhanes. His book, *Aboard a Flying Saucer*, is carefully sub-titled "Non-fiction. A true story of personal experience," and there is even a sketch of the grounded Saucer, which looks not unlike the shell of an oyster. Clarion is not a planet known to astronomers, and the glamorous Mrs Rhanes would seem to be a rather surprising commander for an interplanetary trip—unless, of course, the idea was to attract terrestrial tourists—but the seeds had been well and truly sown.

There followed a detailed account of a Flying Saucerer who landed near Palomar Mountain, in California—though, oddly enough, the staff at the Observatory did not notice anything unusual—and then, in 1954, came Cedric Alling-

Fact or Fiction?

ham's famous *Flying Saucer from Mars*. Whether or not one believes in interplanetary Saucers, there can be no doubt that this particular book is skilfully written, especially as it rejects telepathy, astrology, occultism, and other features generally to be found in such volumes. When I met Allingham in the autumn of the same year, following a lecture which he gave in Tunbridge Wells, he stressed that the book was merely a straightforward account of what had happened to him; he was firm that he really had met a Martian on the Scottish coast, and had even photographed the Saucer concerned.

Yet we must face the facts. Everything we have learned during the last two thousand years and more teaches us that intelligent life on Mars, or anywhere else in the Solar System apart from our own world, is out of the question, the wonderful Saucers which flit through space by creating their own gravity fields, landing occasionally to reveal themselves to persons selected by a Higher Intelligence, are about as plausible as Lucian's horse vultures or Locke's bat-men. We must therefore look for another explanation of the incidents reported by Allingham and others.

The crop of Flying Saucer stories has been less prolific than might have been expected, perhaps because fiction-writers realized that they would be hard pressed to outdo the 'authentic' works. One of the better-known examples is *Star of Ill Omen*, by Dennis Wheatley. Here we have a Mars populated by intelligent bee-beetles and moronic sub-human giants, while the diet consists exclusively of beans.

At any rate, the Flying Saucer cult is completely harmless. It is clearly on the wane now, but it will doubtless last for some time yet, and it will be some years before the various Saucer Clubs send out their last circulars and memoranda.

Locke's hoax and Barnard's comet-seeker are not, of course, unique in scientific history. In recent months an enterprising gentleman in the United States has been busy selling plots of land on the Moon, complete with shooting and fishing rights, and has managed to dispose of over five thousand one-acre plots at a dollar apiece. Such episodes, however, hardly come under the heading of science fiction; and we can leave them with the reflection that there are more fish to be hooked on Earth than on the Moon.

10

"INTERESTING, BUT IMPROBABLE..."

SOME of the best historical novels have made use of loopholes in our knowledge of the past. We have heard how Richard III was the kindly protector of the Princes in the Tower and suffered at the hands of unscrupulous Tudor propagandists; how Bacon wrote Shakespeare (or, alternatively, how Shakespeare wrote Bacon); how Marie Antoinette's son survived the Terror, and so on. Though contrary opinions are usually held, we have no definite proof either way.

Science-fiction writers have done much the same in their own field. It may therefore be of interest to say something about the various weird and wonderful ideas that have been used as backgrounds for novels, short stories, and even films.

Astrology is one old but now outdated favourite. Just after the War there appeared quite a crop of stories in which the future was said to be foretold merely by studying the positions of the stars and planets. What are the true facts about astrological lore?

In the time of Kepler astrology was taken just as seriously as astronomy. Indeed, Kepler himself was a firm believer in it. Basically it may be defined as the superstition of the heavens, with each planet having a marked influence upon each human being. By casting a horoscope, which is merely a chart of the apparent positions of the Sun, Moon, and planets in the sky, an astrologer claims to be able to produce a complete forecast of the future, as well as an accurate summing-up of the character and destiny of the person for whom the horoscope has been drawn. There are still believers in it, just as there are still believers in the Flat Earth.

So long as astrology is confined to circus tents, with Madame Za-Za gazing into her crystal and announcing that her client will meet a dark, handsome man coming over the water some time before next Hallowe'en, there is no harm in it. The only danger is that some credulous person may invest his or her money according to astrological advice, with results that are usually disastrous. Many cases of this are on record.

Occasionally, of course, coincidences happen. Flamsteed, the first Astronomer Royal, was once pestered by an old woman who had lost her laundry and wanted divine help in finding it. To get rid of her, Flamsteed cast a horoscope and told her solemnly that the washing would be found buried at a certain spot in her garden. It was.

Astrological stories have more or less vanished recently, and the only post-1950 example known to me is entitled *Dr Vantrelle and his Horrorscope*, a title which speaks for itself. Stories which involve predictions by supernatural means are, however, more common, and sometimes form a connecting link between astrology and E.S.P. (extrasensory perception).

Another oft-used theme is that of the approaching end of the world. There have been many real panics on this account, most of them due to astrological predictions or to distortions of the Bible. In 1186, for instance, astrologers caused terror all over Europe by announcing that a conjunction of all the known planets in one constellation, Libra, would certainly destroy the world, or would at the very least cause tempests, earthquakes, and widespread chaos. A similar scare occurred in 1524, when Mars, Jupiter, and Saturn lay together in Pisces, and the famous German astrologer Stöfler prophesied that mankind would be overwhelmed by a flood which would make Noah's seem like a small puddle. When the fatal moment passed by with no sign of anything unusual, Stöfler calmly revised his date and predicted the end

"Interesting, but Improbable . . ."

of the world for 1588. By that time he was, of course, dead, and so had no chance to amend his calculations still further.

The greatest panic of all was that of 1843. William Miller, a Massachusetts farmer, announced that his studies of the Bible had proved that the world would end at midnight on March 21, and added that he had been granted divine permission to tell his fellow-men what was in store for them. The Millerite movement spread widely across the American continent, and many believers even sold their farms, cutting down their trees and abandoning their crops. A great comet, which appeared in the heavens without warning, made the confusion still worse. On the evening of March 21 crowds gathered on hill-tops, while Miller himself spent the last hours praying in his farmhouse. Nothing happened—not even a shower of meteors. Miller changed the date to March 21, 1844, but again met with no success. He was so disappointed that he died soon afterwards.

Collisions with comets have also caused alarm. In 1773 the approach of a small and harmless comet created a panic in France, and certain opportunist ministers of the Church took care to sell seats in Paradise to the wealthier members of their congregations. Actually, the chances of our being hit by a comet, an asteroid, or anything else are so small that they can be neglected; nor is there much chance that the Solar System will be invaded by a wandering dark star.

End-of-the-world stories are of many types. Some, such as Wells's *The Star*, involve only extensive damage and loss of life; others tell how the world is blown apart by an atomic explosion or battered to pieces by collision with some solid body. Philip Lathom, in a most ingenious short story called *The Xi Effect*, describes the disastrous shrinking of the fundamental constant of the universe. And Olaf Stapledon, in *Last and First Men*, tells how mankind saves itself by migrating to Venus in good time. Unfortunately the theme cannot be made at all credible, for the simple reason that the Earth has not been destroyed—we are still living on it.

Matthew Shiel's *The Purple Cloud*, published in 1901, is

not a true end-of-the-world story, but it does involve the almost complete depopulation of the globe. Adam Jeffson, the central character, returns from a North Polar expedition to find that humanity has been destroyed by cyanide gas emitted during a tremendous volcanic eruption. For twenty years he wanders alone, burning cities as he comes to them, until in Constantinople he finds that one of the Sultan's daughters has somehow survived. Not unnaturally, he marries her, despite the lack of any officiating clergyman, and vows that he will found a new race.

As long ago as 1825 Mary Wollstonecraft Shelley—best known for her *Frankenstein*—wrote a book called *The Last Man*, describing how humanity was destroyed by plague until only one hapless male was left. This idea has been used many times since, but more ingenious is that employed by J. J. Connington in *Nordenholt's Million*, published shortly before the War. Here the decimation is due to the failure of all natural crops, so that mankind simply starves. Led by Nordenholt, the 'strong man,' some thousands of people manage to husband their supplies until conditions become normal once more, giving them the chance to rebuild.

Shifting a planet in its path has also had a good many supporters. I first came across this idea some time before the War, when the now-defunct boys' magazine *Chums* carried a story which combined planet-moving with the usual Menace to Earth. This time the Earth is invaded by short-tempered B.E.M.'s from Dione, the fourth satellite of Saturn, and the terrestrial retort is to build a huge magnet that wrenches Saturn from its path and plunges it into the Sun—rings, satellites, B.E.M.'s, and all. I remember, too, a tale by Murray Roberts, in the *Modern Boy*, in which the red planet Nuvius is drawn earthward by Professor Flaznagel's remarkable machine. An earlier adult novel on the same lines was, of course, Laurie's *Conquest of the Moon*. But when we calculate the force necessary to disturb a planet in its orbit, we soon find that any such thing is absolutely out of the question.

Several planet-moving stories appeared in 1951 as a result of Dr Immanuel Velikovsky's *Worlds in Collision*, published during the previous year. This profound work was a grand medley of distorted religion, so-called science, and pure fantasy. It described how the supernatural events related in the Old Testament, including the Flood, were caused by encounters with a comet which later changed, in some unspecified way, into the planet Venus. Unfortunately a comet is not a solid body; it is made up of numerous small particles enveloped in a cloud of tenuous gas, and even the largest comet is of negligible mass compared with Venus or even an asteroid. Velikovsky went on to show how the Earth's rotation was actually stopped for several hours, causing hosts of men to be asphyxiated by meteorite smoke. Even now I am not sure whether his book was meant to be taken seriously.

Perpetual motion, another method of getting something for nothing, has been used in many stories and has been the subject of countless experiments. Like the circle-squarer, the perpetual-motion enthusiast is generally a harmless crank who is firmly convinced that he is on the verge of a great discovery. The classic case is that of Johann Bessler, better known as Orffyreus, who is said to have built a self-revolving wheel and to have had it tested in 1717, though he was wise enough to destroy it before it could be thoroughly examined by competent experts. He has had imitators in plenty; only a few months ago I had a letter from an Austrian investigator who claims to have constructed a perpetual-motion machine based on permanent magnets.

Here, again, there are endless opportunities. The usual plot concerns a scientist who discovers the long-lost secret and then meets with opposition from the emperors of Big Business. There can be no doubt that a perpetual-motion device would cause a good deal of chaos in the world of finance, since it would provide a source of unlimited power, and if skilfully handled such a theme can be most entertaining—so long as we remember that perpetual-motion machines exist only in the imaginations of those who write about them.

Perpetual motion is said to have been well known to the inhabitants of Atlantis, the wonderful continent which was the home of advanced beings with superhuman powers until it sank beneath the waves in a single day. The Atlantis cult is far from dead, and the recent Flying Saucer craze has given it a new lease of life, since it appears that the Martians have strong family ties with the ancient Atlantean lords of light. Unfortunately, geological research proves that the mystical continent never existed in any such form.

However, the idea is most attractive, and Atlantis makes its entrance now and again. In *The Maracot Deep*, published in 1929, Sir Arthur Conan Doyle relates how Dr Maracot and his companions descend to the ocean floor in a steel sphere, only to be stranded there when their cables are nipped through by a gigantic lobster-like creature. Fortunately they are rescued by a man in a glassy suit, who leads them to Atlantis—now an enclosed city beneath the seabed. After meeting many interesting characters, including the local Devil, Dr Maracot and his friends return to the ocean surface and are picked up by a passing ship.

Having satisfied themselves as to the former existence of Atlantis, nineteenth-century lovers of Ancient Lore turned their attention to the Egyptian Pyramids and established what was virtually a new religion. Pyramidology was even supported by the then Astronomer Royal for Scotland, Professor Piazzi Smyth, and it still has a few followers. The cult is based upon the dimensions of the Great Pyramid, with its precise orientation and remarkable passages, and devotees claim that by means of measurements it can be shown that the pyramid builders possessed knowledge of the past, present, and future unsurpassed by Solomon or anybody else. The religion also includes more than its fair proportion of circle-squarers.

It is quite true to say that some of the Egyptians were scientifically in advance of their time, and it is even possible, though improbable, that they had solved the secret of the refracting telescope. On the other hand, most of the 'mystery' surrounding Ancient Egypt was deliberately created by the priests themselves. They were more learned than their fellow-countrymen, and by pretending that they knew the answers to all the riddles of the universe they could keep a tight hold upon the reins of power. They had sound knowledge of positional astronomy, and the accuracy of the pyramid orientation is truly marvellous, but the priests were so astrology-ridden that they could make no progress in other directions.

The Lost Knowledge story always begins with the discovery of an ancient scroll, usually buried in a tomb, and goes on to describe the impact of Atlantean or Egyptian wisdom upon the modern world. There is plenty of scope, but the theme is seldom used nowadays, mainly because pyramidology and Atlantis worship are no longer studied except by an admittedly vocal minority.

It is only one step from a sunken continent to a complete sunken world, and this brings us at once to the much-played idea of a hollow earth. Jules Verne's *Journey to the Centre of Earth* remains the supreme story of the depths, but there have been others, and several appeared during the nineteenth century as a result of a weird theory put forward, quite seriously, by Captain John Cleves Symmes of the United States Army.

From all accounts, Symmes was a brave and capable soldier. He joined the Army in 1802, with the rank of ensign, and distinguished himself in several battles. As a scientist he was, perhaps, rather less capable. He believed the Earth to be made up of five hollow, concentric spheres, with space between each, and habitable upon both the concave and convex surfaces. He also thought that there were entrances at each Pole, through which passed seals, whales, and other sea-creatures, and in 1823 he even tried to persuade Congress to send a naval expedition to test his theory, apparently because he thought that once the ships broke through the icy barrier of the polar sea, they would find a warm, equable land surrounding the entrance itself. He was bitterly disappointed when Congress rejected the proposed expedition, but he had at least the satisfaction of knowing that twenty-five Members supported him.

Symmes first drew attention to himself in 1818, when he started to bombard universities and technical colleges with leaflets and memoranda 'proving' the truth of his concentric-sphere theory. The first story based upon the hypothesis appeared shortly afterwards, and was entitled *Symzonia*, which is a sure indication that it was inspired by the work of Captain Symmes. It was by another Captain, Adam Seaborn, and told how he and his crew sailed over the rim of the world until they arrived at an inner continent, lit by two dim suns and two equally dim moons. The inhabitants were white, and had established a veritable Utopia. Their ruler was the Best Man, elected because of his outstanding personal qualities, and greed and poverty were unknown. Not unnaturally, the Symzonians were afraid that visitors from the outside world might cause trouble, and Seaborn and his crew were sent kindly but firmly on their way.

Seaborn's tale makes rather difficult reading, but it certainly makes one think. The idea of having a Best Man for ruler is enough to disturb the artificial calm of any professional politician of the twentieth century, and this must also have been so during the nineteenth.

An earlier hollow-earth story is Baron Ludwig Holberg's *A Journey to the World Under-Ground* (1742). Here we find a complete solar system beneath the terrestrial crust, with a sun in the middle and several planets revolving round it. The central character, Nicholas Klimius, encounters a huge bird which carries him to the planet Nazar. Nazar turns out to be a curious world; there are trees with human heads and other unusual features, while the Nazarians themselves despise wealth and regard a quick-brained man as moronic. On another planet, Mutak, invalids are put into prison and criminals into hospitals, while on the inner surface of the

"Interesting, but Improbable . . ." 129

Earth there exists a race of intelligent apes. William Bradshaw's *Goddess of Atvatabar* (1892) is obviously drawn from Holberg. Here, too, we have the central sun, plant-animals such as birds equipped with roots, and mechanical ostriches. The central sun appears once more in *Tarzan at the Earth's Core*, by Edgar Rice Burroughs. Tarzan the Ape-Man is justly famous, but he is clearly out of his element in Pellucidar, the inner world peopled by prehistoric monsters and sub-men, so that this particular book is far from being one of Burroughs' more successful efforts. Tarzan is more at home in his native jungle.

Verne's excepted, the most ingenious of the hollow-earth stories is W. N. Harben's *Land of the Changing Sun*, published in 1894. It is perhaps wrong to class it with the others, since the two explorers, Johnson and Thorndyke, discover not a true inner world, but merely a cavern a hundred miles across, lying well below the bed of the sea. The local 'sun' is artificial, and has been produced by means of electrical control. Unfortunately, Thorndyke discovers that the roof has begun to leak, and the story ends with the hasty evacuation of the wonderful cavern.

Very few 'stories of the depths' have been produced since 1900, and now that we have at least a fair knowledge of conditions below the terrestrial crust it is clear that no such stories can be made even remotely plausible. However, there are still a few earnest folk who refuse to believe that the world is a sphere. The Flat Earthers seem to have been discouraged by recent photographs taken from high-altitude rockets, showing the curvature so plainly that not even the most hardened Flatearthologist can attribute it to refraction, but there is still some support for the idea that the Earth itself is the inside of a hollow sphere. This cult is centred in Germany, and in 1933 an experiment was actually carried out in an attempt to prove or disprove it.

The prime mover was an engineer named Mengering, who had some connexions with the City Council of Magdeburg. He became converted to the hollow-sphere school of

I

thought, and reasoned that a rocket sent vertically 'upward' to a sufficient height should end its career by landing in the Antipodes. A rocket was duly built and fired. It rose to a height of six feet, and then crashed, after which no further experiments were made. Mengering's views upon this disappointing result are not, fortunately, on record.

Yet another idea which has given fiction-writers considerable scope is that of calling up our friends on Mars, Venus, or the Moon. So far as I know, the first serious suggestion as to how this might be done was made about a hundred and fifty years ago by one of the greatest mathematicians of all time, Karl Friedrich Gauss. Gauss wanted to produce geometrical patterns in Siberia by planting pine-trees in a regular pattern. He reasoned that since geometry is natural and is not man-made, the sudden appearance of an isosceles triangle would tell the Martians that they were being signalled. It was assumed, of course, that the inhabitants of the Red World were equipped with powerful telescopes.

The idea was modified by Littrow, of Austria, who transferred it to the Sahara Desert and replaced the pine-trees with fire-filled ditches. However, neither scheme appeared practicable, and neither was actually tried.

Charles Cros, a French inventor, approached the problem in a different light. In 1869 he produced a book, *Moyens de Communication avec les Planètes*, which is well worth reading as an example of really crazy thinking. Cros planned to build a very long-focus mirror with a diameter equal to that of Europe, and to focus the solar rays upon the Martian deserts, scorching them just as a burning-glass can be used to scorch a piece of paper. He went on to add that by judicious swinging of the mirror it would even be possible to write words. (I have often wondered just what words he proposed to transmit.) Cros did his best to persuade the French Government to finance the scheme, and spent months in bombarding Ministers and Departments with letters, memoranda, petitions, and pamphlets, but officialdom refused to co-operate.

"Interesting, but Improbable . . ."

I have come across two stories based on Cros' idea. One of them is French, and was written in 1882 by Pierre Lecœur, an author about whom I have been unable to find out anything further. It describes the building of a giant mirror and how it is destroyed when the Sun's rays strike it, killing the hapless inventor in the process. The other story is American, and a rather obvious copy of Lecœur's.

The only related stories of modern times concern that much-publicized and quite impracticable object, the Space-Mirror. Just after the end of the War newspaper reports stated that Hitler's scientists had been engaged in the construction of a large reflecting mirror which was to be set in orbit round the Earth, with the object of focusing solar heat on to Allied cities and setting them alight. Actually, the idea was first thought out by Oberth and his colleagues, but there is not the slightest chance of its ever being built, and certainly the Nazi workers had wasted no time on it.

The development of radio opened up a new field, and wireless contact with Mars became widely discussed. In 1924 the Post Office went so far as to accept a telegram for a Martian address, though they refused to guarantee its safe arrival and were prudent enough to charge 1s. 6d. a word to transmit it. When Mars approached the Earth in 1939, a team of radio amateurs on Long Island sent out a message in the Morse code, following it with ten minutes of a jazz-band. No reply was received, and it is logical to assume that the jazz-band alone would have been sufficient to make intelligent Martians realize that the Earth is best left alone.

Countless stories have been written on the theme of messages from Mars, and there was a time, just before the War, when most space stories began in some such way. More recently the trend has been to establish mental contact first, and leave more mundane methods severely alone. In 1954 I even attended a lecture at Caxton Hall addressed by a Mr Aetherius, who lives on Saturn—where the Intergalactic Council holds its board meetings—and has been given special permission to contact Earthmen by means of direct voice. At question-time, I asked how long the Venusians had been in touch with Earth, and was given the firm answer: "180 million years." According to my calculations, this would take us back to the Triassic Period, and it seems hardly likely that the Venusians would travel millions of miles just to exchange greetings with a stegosaurus; but Aetherius was unable to explain further, as he was called away by an urgent message from Saturn.

A recent book on the subject is called *Venus Speaks*. This is by an author who signs himself [squiggle] and who is, we are told, the chief scientist of Venus. Further discussion of it here would be out of place.

In any case, it is always dangerous to accuse anyone of being a crank. Galileo was held up to scorn when he first announced that he had discovered four moons revolving round Jupiter; Dalton, of atomic-theory fame, was similarly attacked, and more modern examples of ridiculed but subsequently justified pioneers are Ziolkovsky, Goddard, and Oberth. Now and then, however, one comes across the real Crazy Gang, and I cannot resist quoting one example of really remarkable reasoning. In 1952 the British Interplanetary Society received a letter stating that Flying Saucers come from the planet Strorp, 27,000 light-years from the Earth, and that a party of researchers had been in touch with this interesting planet "through the medium of Kelmic energy." It was added that men from Strorp had established a base on the Moon, and had decided that since we are so obviously incapable of governing our own world, it would be unwise to allow us to land on any other.

Normally such letters are ignored, but this one was really too good to miss. In a reply it was pointed out that the author must have been the victim of a hoax, since more reliable sources of information, still on the secret list, proved that "the Saucers are not from Strorp, but from the much closer planet Ploop, only 3,560 light-years away . . ."

11

MUTANTS AND ROBOTS

The idea of robots, or mechanical men, is by no means new. This is understandable, since there is nothing particularly difficult in building a piece of machinery in the form of a human figure. On the other hand, the 'mutant' theme is much more modern, and has been used as much as any basic plot in science fiction, apart from the purely interplanetary one.

What is a mutant? In Latin, *mutare* means 'to change,' and a mutant may be defined as a being which differs from its parents in some important way. Generation after generation these tiny alterations mount up, so that the 'mutation' becomes obvious. Practical experiments have been made with regard to lowly forms of life, but in human beings the life-span of each individual is so extended that mutations, even if they are going on, are not appreciable.

The story-teller, then, must speed up the process. The obvious way to do so is by means of radiation. The dangers of radioactivity are known to every one, and it is true to say that the worst part of the Hiroshima atom-bomb was not the blast itself, but the delayed effects which led to a hideous death for the luckless men, women, and children who had been in the lethal zone. While it is true that we have no evidence that exposure to radiation can cause mutation, a definite doubt must remain; we are meddling with forces that we do not properly understand.

Up to now our experiments have been on too small a scale to form a real menace except in a comparatively localized area. The popular idea that they have affected the weather, for instance, is based on very slender evidence. (In 1954 Britain had an unusually cool and wet summer; parts of Russia suffered a drought and a heat-wave; and both countries blamed it on The Bomb.) But the effects of radioactive contamination are cumulative; and now that regular tests are being carried out both east and west of the Iron Curtain, the radioactive content of the air has already been increased perceptibly. It has, moreover, been calculated that the supply of bombs now in existence would suffice to destroy all life on the Earth. Statesmen in general consider this to be a sign of real progress.

In 1930, just before the pulps had begun to make themselves notorious, John Taine wrote a story called *The Iron Star*. It describes how a curious meteor falls in Africa, made up of a metal christened Asterium which sends out deadly radiation. The radiation does not kill, but it causes degeneration of the human body, so that the victims change slowly but surely into brutish, ape-like creatures. The menace is removed by a party of scientists who play X-rays upon the meteor, causing it to blow up.

Taine, in ordinary life Professor E. T. Bell, of the California Institute of Technology, was well equipped to write such a novel. It is skilfully done, and is good entertainment. Unfortunately, the Gloom School appeared on the scene shortly afterwards, and the modern mutant is always repulsive and bloodthirsty, generally possessing several ears and (if female) a few extra breasts. Moreover, mutants are invariably telepathic. No mutant is of the aristocracy unless he has unlimited powers of telepathy, and the stories written around this theme must number thousands.

There is a good deal of evidence in favour of the genuineness of telepathy, even when we make due allowance for coincidences. The experiments on the subject of extra-sensory perception (E.S.P.) conducted by the American scientist Dr Rhine are so well known that it is unnecessary to discuss them here. But the picking up of an idea or tune, or the correct guessing of a concealed card, is compara-

Mutants and Robots

tively very minor. The telepaths of science fiction are true thought-readers, who can probe a man's mind and draw upon the whole store of his knowledge. So far, at least, any such process is beyond our understanding.

What would be the popular reaction to a genuine telepath whose supernormal powers could not be doubted? Distrust, I think, followed by open animosity and fear, and ending in a witch-hunt. Public orators inside and outside governments would be in a particularly bad way if opposed by a telepath; they might even have to submit to the hideous fate of having to say what they really think.

This point is driven home by Sir Arthur Ronald Fraser in his *The Flying Draper*, first published in 1924. Professor Codling, the central character, has tired of biochemistry and has turned to the life of an obscure draper. Unfortunately for him, he has a "cosmic consciousness," and is aware of ages that have found a climax in his person. Moreover, he can fly, and he is in every sense a man apart. Inevitably he suffers for his super-normal powers; he is persecuted by the mob, and in the end succumbs to the forces of the world.

Very different, though with an underlying common factor, is Olaf Stapledon's *Odd John*, sub-titled, "A Story between Jest and Earnest." Here we meet a boy possessed of strange powers, who manages to collect others of his kind and to found a fantastic island colony, only to be destroyed in the end by the fear and animosity of "normal" men. They die voluntarily; their powers could have saved them easily enough had they been prepared to take life, but in their view no such action was justifiable. *Odd John* is a remarkable book, and is outstanding among stories of mutants and supernormals. It first appeared in 1935.

Professor Codling and Odd John are enlightened beings, despite their powers, but this is not true of the Gloom mutants. There seems no reason to suppose that a telepath should misuse his gifts, but this does not seem to occur to most writers, though there are, of course, notable exceptions.

Cosmic rays are often used to produce mutation, and we

have to admit that these rays are still something of a mystery to science. We know what they are, and strictly speaking they are not rays at all, but high-velocity atomic nuclei. On the other hand, we know nothing at all about their origin, apart from the fact that they come from deep space, and we are almost equally ignorant as to their effects upon living tissue. This is largely because we cannot study them properly so long as we stay at or near ground-level. The primary particles are blocked by the atmosphere, and we do not start to meet them much below an altitude of 45,000 feet. By the time we have risen to thirty miles we are in the thick of them, but one cannot jack up a complete laboratory to such an altitude, and so far our researches have been carried out mainly by rockets which carry instruments. It is clear that cosmic rays are not immediately lethal, since animals have been sent up into the main zone and have returned unharmed, but long-continued exposure to them may be dangerous. Nor is there definite proof that the rays will not cause mutation, even though the weight of such evidence as we have is against any such thing.

A typical Gloom story involves men who depart for Mars or the Moon, suffer from cosmic rays, and return home hideously mis-shapen and mentally twisted. It seems a pity, and it is quite unjustifiable.

Closely allied with telepathy is the idea that human minds can be controlled by alien creatures from another world or another dimension. This theme can be found even in one of the lesser Wells stories, *Star Begotten*. Wells, of course, had his own way of dealing with the situation, and even if *Star Begotten* does not rank among his best fantasies—it was written at a comparatively late stage in his career—it is told with much of the power so evident in his early science fiction. It is in sharp contrast to a 'horror' story of soul transference, M. Renard's *New Bodies for Old*, published in 1923. Here we have a whole series of transferences, ending in a remarkable climax when the soul of the villain takes possession of a motor-car. A driving-test examiner once told me that it is not uncommon for applicants (usually members of the fair sex) to accuse their cars of being possessed of the Devil, but I still maintain that this kind of theme is suited only to farce. Nor do I class it as genuine science fiction.

Robots are in a different category. Although it would be difficult, risky, and undesirable to make any attempt to produce human mutation, a robot is merely a piece of machinery built in the form of a man, and can be assembled at any time. Even speech can be added by means of a gramophone record or something equally obvious. Many robots have, in fact, been made for the stage and screen.

Fictional robots are, of course, more advanced. It is held that if a mechanical man is made to greater and greater perfection there will eventually come a time when the 'brain' will acquire what is loosely termed a 'soul,' so that even if it can neither feel, eat, nor sleep, the robot will cease to be a mere piece of machinery and will assume a character and personality of its own. One or two notable short stories have been written upon this theme, a particularly clever example being Peter Phillips' *Unknown Quantity*, published not long ago in a science-fiction anthology.

So far as we know at present, the acquisition of a 'soul' by any machine, man-shaped or otherwise, is pure fantasy. It is, however, far from impossible that robots will be developed to the point of carrying out useful tasks, and even making intelligent conversation. There are already robot chess-players, though not so ferocious as that described in 1893 by Ambrose Bierce in *Moxon's Master*, which was so annoyed at being checkmated that it leaned forward and strangled its human opponent in an iron grip.

The talking robot is not so absurd as it sounds. Even an automatic calculating-machine may be said to have a brain of a sort; a century ago anyone who suggested leaving mathematics to a machine would have been considered an automatic candidate for the nearest asylum. When the first talking robots are produced there may well be a general outcry, and perhaps even the formation of a N.S.P.C.R.

(National Society for the Prevention of Cruelty to Robots); but they will still be machines, and once we overstep the boundaries of science, we are back to life creation and Type 1 fiction.

A favourite plot involves the development of robots which become intelligent enough to turn upon their makers, finally assuming control of the whole planet. My only comment here is that no robot could possibly make a worse job of world-government than *homo sapiens* has done.

It is, of course, possible to class Mr Hyde, of *Dr Jekyll and Mr Hyde* fame, as a mutant of sorts, though the connexion is rather remote.

One of the cleverest robot books known to me is *I, Robot*, by "Isaac Asimov," published in 1952. This is a collection of short stories tracing the development of robots during the twenty-first century. We begin with the non-talking, definitely mechanical variety, and end with a being so human in appearance that nobody can be sure whether it is a robot or not. Novels of this kind form a kind of bridge between Types 1 and 2. They are not pure fantasy, but neither are they even remotely possible at the moment.

A robot with a soul is no more probable than the B.E.M. of the pulps. Perhaps this is just as well for mere mortals such as ourselves.

12

TIME TRAVEL

TRAVELLING through space is becoming a real possibility. Within a few centuries at most we may be fairly confident that men will have covered the quarter-million miles to the Moon and perhaps the few tens of millions of miles to Mars and Venus. Yet what are the chances of our learning how to travel through that intangible other dimension, time?

Our conventional time-scale is based upon the movements of the Earth. Our planet spins in approximately 24 hours, and revolves round the Sun in about 365 days, which gives us our 'day' and 'year'; the Moon's period of revolution has similarly led to the 'month.' It is clear that these units are of no importance in the cosmos as a whole. To a Martian the 'year' would be 687 of our 24-hour periods, so that an Earthman of twenty-one would be a mere boy of eleven of Mars,[1] while a 'day' on Jupiter is equal to only ten terrestrial hours. Our division of the day into hours, minutes, and seconds is even less fundamental, convenient though it may be for everyday purposes.

Jules Verne demonstrated this in *Round the World in Eighty Days*. Phileas Fogg agrees to travel right round the globe in exactly eighty days, but since he goes from west to east, he gains a day without realizing it. This, however, is in no sense 'time travel'; it is merely a trick based upon our own conventional units.

In any case, we do not really understand 'time.' When did the universe begin? "Judging from the known facts about the age of the Earth, we can estimate that the universe

---

[1] In New York there is even a clock regulated to keep Martian Mean Time!

was created some eight thousand million years ago," according to one authority. Yet the universe as we know it must have evolved from matter already in existence, either as a sort of super-atom or as a cloud of tenuous gas distributed throughout all space. When was this matter itself created? No matter how far back we go, we can picture a still earlier period. Belief in an absolute 'creation,' before which there was nothing, is of no help; when did the nothingness begin? The problem is too fundamental for our reeling minds to appreciate, and we are equally unable to picture a period of time that has no end.

Travelling through time seems at first glance to be a total impossibility, but it provides the fiction-writer with immense scope, and the methods used in different stories are most ingenious. Undoubtedly the greatest of such tales is *The Time Machine*, written by H. G. Wells in 1895. Wells used the time-travelling device to examine social conditions in the Earth of the future, but the book is unquestionably science fiction. It is a remarkable work, doubly so since it was a first novel by a then unknown writer.

As in his later fantasies, Wells says very little about the construction and operation of his wonderful machine. We are merely told how the Time Traveller sits upon the saddle, reverses some switches, and hurtles headlong into the future:

> I am afraid I cannot convey the peculiar sensations of time travelling. They are excessively unpleasant. There is a feeling exactly like that one has on a switchback—of a helpless headlong motion. I felt the same horrible anticipation, too, of an imminent smash. As I put on pace, night followed day like the flapping of a black wing. The dim suggestion of the laboratory seemed presently to fall away from me, and I saw the sun hopping swiftly across the sky, leaping it every minute, and every minute marking a day. . . .

At last the Time Traveller arrives in the Earth of the future, where he finds that mankind had become divided into two distinct races. There are the day-people, the charming, futile

Time Travel

Eloi, and the hideous creatures of the night, the Morlocks. The picture of decadent humanity devoid of all ambition or courage is not a pleasant one, but we are left with an uneasy feeling that it might become reality.

The Time Traveller's journey is not over. Escaping at last from the Morlocks, he speeds on for countless ages until he reaches a period when men have vanished from the Earth, and only monstrous crab-like creatures inhabit the dying world. Small wonder that he comes back, only to undertake a second journey and vanish for ever into the future—or the past.

Fantasy, perhaps; but fantasy that has seldom been surpassed, and *The Time Machine* remains a classic of its kind. It established Wells in the eyes of his contemporaries, and paved the way for the other novels that were to flow from his pen.

Nor must we forget his *New Accelerator*, one of the "Twelve Stories and a Dream." Here we have a remarkable drug invented by Professor Gibberne, capable of slowing down 'time' for anyone who swallows the contents of the phial, so that each second seems extended into minutes. This tale shows Wells in the rôle of humorist, and is certainly one of the rare examples of a really funny science-fiction story.

Most of the writers who attempted to emulate *The Time Machine* failed dismally, chiefly because they tried to introduce scientific details of the machine itself and thereby destroyed the illusion of plausibility. Creating a spaceship is all very well, since even if we cannot yet build one in reality we do at least have a sound idea of how it can be done; but the principle of any time machine is completely beyond us.

Failing mechanical devices, some authors turned to the 'time-warp,' a delightfully nebulous term which can be construed to mean practically anything. Suppose that we regard time as an 'ever-rolling stream,' and draw it as a straight line, as in the diagram, with a certain interval between Event A and Event B. By curving the line, as in the second diagram, we can bring A and B closer together, so that we can cheat Nature by taking a short cut. We have, in

theory, solved the problem of time travel in a single easy lesson. The trouble is that we have not the remotest idea of how such a thing can be done, even if we stretch a great many points and suppose that it can be done at all.

Still, time-warps of various kinds provide a useful method of permitting our dauntless heroes to leap back and forth, breakfasting in the Tudor period and having lunch served by a robot of A.D. 3000. What usually happens is that the traveller becomes stranded, and has to live out his life in some period of history to which he is peculiarly unfitted. Some of the time machines are purely mechanical, as Wells's was; some of the warp stories involve mental waves, and others employ principles intelligible only to the magazine addict. However, some really good stories have been produced. Not long ago the Sunday *Observer* ran a competition for short-story writers, now published as a collection under the title *A.D. 2000*, and the winning tale was a time-travel one, treated in a semi-humorous vein which came as a refreshing change from the general Gloom.

Another method of reaching the future is by putting the time traveller into a state of suspended animation. Wells did so in *When the Sleeper Wakes*, first published in 1899, and issued in revised form in 1910 as *The Sleeper Awakes*, but to me the supreme story on this theme is *The Man in Asbestos*, written by—of all people—Stephen Leacock.

Leacock, in ordinary life a very serious and eminent Professor of Political Economy at McGill University, in Canada, will always be remembered for his humorous books such as *Nonsense Novels, Winsome Winnie, Behind the Beyond, Moonbeams from the Larger Lunacy,* and *Literary Lapses*. Each of these sent a gale of laughter round the world, and each is as mirth-provoking to-day as when first written. His story of the future occurs in *Nonsense Novels,* and may well have been a parody of Wells's *Time Machine*.

The story begins with an attempt by the narrator to "fall asleep for two or three hundred years at least, and wake and find myself in the marvel world of the future." The method of producing suspended animation is simply to eat some pie and doughnuts and then to read a series of comic papers, followed by the desperate expedient of plunging into the editorial page of the London Weekly *Times*.

> It was in a way clear, straight suicide, but I did it . . . I could feel my senses leaving me. I fell into a sleep, the deep immeasurable sleep in which the very existence of the outer world was hushed. Dimly I could feel the days go by, then the years, and then the long passage of the centuries . . .

Leacock's picture of the future Earth differs from that of Wells. Men have learned how to eliminate Death, and Food, and Change, thus practically getting rid of Events; work has been finished, and the weather has been killed by turning the forces of Nature against one another, making the sky grey and the sea gum-coloured and gelatinous. Education is given by a series of operations, so that men's stomachs are literally full of learning, and international disputes—if they occur—are settled by the use of a slot-machine. Clothes are made of asbestos, and sex has been banished along with travel, entertainment, and other features of the breathless twentieth century.

Really funny science-fiction stories can be counted on the fingers of one hand, but every would-be Verne or Wells should read *The Man in Asbestos* as part of his literary education. Even so, there is a substratum of cold common sense, as is so often the case in Leacock's work.

A device often used by more conventional writers is to allow the hero to live his allotted span in a series of jerks, separated by vast periods of suspended animation. This 'time-jumping' has interesting results, since by going into cold storage for fifty or sixty years at a time one can easily make the acquaintance of one's own great-great-grand-children. I once read a short story in which the idea was developed in an ingenious manner, but unfortunately the literary style was very poor, and I cannot even remember the name of the author. Needless to say, time-jumping can be done in one direction only, and there is always the difficulty of how to make a story of A.D. 5000 available to a reader of A.D. 1956.

One good time-travel story of the pre-pulp era was E. V. Odle's *The Clockwork Man* (1923). Here we have a being of A.D. 8000 who arrives suddenly in our own century, involuntarily and unannounced. We learn that he comes from an age in which men have incorporated machines into their bodies in order to improve human efficiency, and that his own abrupt leap backward in time is due to a defect in his clock. The story ends when he is about to return to his own period, and goes to shake hands with his 1923 friend—but his clock is still erratic, and "they missed each other by several days."

Time stories have become very common in recent years. Edmond Hamilton has produced two of exceptional interest. In *City at World's End*, a super-atomic bomb blows a complete Middle Western town into the far future, while in *The Star Kings* a scientist of A.D. 200,000 manages to exchange minds with an undistinguished twentieth-century American clerk. F. C. Rayer, in *Tomorrow Sometimes Comes*, has pictured "reversible time." All these are frankly fantastic, and of Type 1, but they succeed because they are skilfully written. I again stress that I would be the last to condemn fiction merely because it *is* of Type 1.

Yet another method used now and then is to move at very high velocity, so that one's time is slowed down. There is practical scientific proof that this kind of thing can happen, so that the theme is perfectly legitimate—apart from the practical difficulties of accelerating to anything like the speed of light.

The first inkling of any such time effect was given by Albert Einstein. Einstein, the Newton of the twentieth century, will be remembered by scientists as long as the human race endures, even if his death in 1954 did cause much less of a stir than the sixth marriage of a Hollywood film actress which took place during the same month. Einstein's idea was summed up by the author of a famous limerick:

> There was a young lady named Bright,
> Who travelled much faster than light.
>   She started one day
>   In the Relative way,
> And came back the previous night.

It is impossible to explain the Theory of Relativity in non-mathematical language, but at least something can be said about its effects. Light, as we know, travels at the immense speed of 186,000 miles a second. Could a rocket be accelerated to near this 'optic velocity,' strange things would start to happen to its time and mass. The mass would increase, and the time-scale would slow down. Dr L. R. Shepherd, former Chairman of the British Interplanetary Society, once calculated that if a ship could leave for the star Procyon, some 50 million million miles away, and move at 99·9 per cent. of the velocity of light, it would make the round trip in 21 years of Earth time. To the rocket's crew, however, the period would seem to be only 3 years; the whole idea of time would be slowed down, and the crew would return home to find themselves younger than the nieces and nephews they had left behind. A grand tour of the universe could therefore result in the travellers returning to a dead or dying Earth.

This is not mere theory: it can be proved. Mention has already been made of the strange high-velocity particles known as cosmic rays, which bombard the Earth from outer space. As the cosmic-ray particles smash into the upper air they create secondary particles known as mu mesons.

K

As these mu mesons are formed at altitudes of ten miles and over, and last for only about one two-millionth of a second each, they should not live long enough to reach ground-level before disintegrating; yet many of them do. They are travelling at almost the speed of light, and their time is slowed down relative to ours, so that on our scale they last for longer than two-millionths of a second.

At optic velocity itself, 186,000 miles a second, time stands still. In other words, such a speed is impossible to attain. There is, moreover, the mass effect to be considered; at the speed of light, the mass of a solid body would become infinite. This mass effect also has been proved experimentally, in this case by studying the motions of Mercury, a planet which is small enough and quick-moving enough to show indications of the Einstein phenomenon.

It is interesting to speculate as to what would happen to a rocket travelling at greater than optic speed, always supposing that we could find some way of avoiding the mass effect. Would it travel backward in time, so that the voyagers would return to be greeted by the trumpetings of a mammoth or the scream of a scolosaurus? The sudden materialization of a vacuum-suited space-man among the ranks of the Athenians at Marathon, for instance, would yield material for a story light-hearted in vein.

Stories set wholly in the future are also common. Arthur Clarke's *Earthlight* is an excellent example. The scene is the Moon, the period the not-too-distant future when the lunar world has been conquered and colonized, and since the scientific details are as accurate as they can be made, the reader will be left with a real impression of what life on the Moon will be like. In general, however, stories of the future describe the hackneyed space-captains voyaging between impossible planets, moving "much faster than light" and hobnobbing with evil spiders, plant-men, and intangible telepaths, while the dumb blonde in attendance proves to be a member of the Intergalactic Police Corps. In Ray Bradbury's *Fahrenheit 451* we enter a nightmare age in which firemen are concerned with destroying books rather than in quenching flames.

One of the first time-travel stories must have been Louis Mercier's *Memoirs of the Year Two Thousand Five Hundred*, which appeared as long ago as 1771, and in which the central character goes to sleep and wakes up in the Paris of A.D. 2500. Samuel Madden's *The Reign of George VI, 1900-1925* was published eight years earlier, but can hardly be regarded as science fiction. It is, in fact, rather difficult to decide what is science fiction and what is not. A case can be made out even for George Orwell's *1984*.

A novel theory put forward in recent years by F. Hoyle, of Cambridge, alters the general picture of the future to some extent. Hoyle avoids the 'beginnings and endings' difficulty by supposing that matter is being created all the time. On older theories, the universe is likened to a clock which is slowly running down; Hoyle prefers to compare it with a clock which is being continuously re-wound. He does not, of course, suggest that a star or planet can appear suddenly out of nothingness. The rate of creation of matter is slow enough to be undetectable even by means of the most sensitive instruments that we can ever hope to devise, but Nature is never in a hurry.

Hoyle's theory is completely unproved, and, in fact, it is probably incapable of proof, so that we shall never know whether it is true or false. It is at any rate an intriguing possibility, and there is just a chance that it may lead to a better understanding of 'time,' in which case the story-tellers will not be slow to exploit it.

One fact, however, is certain: whether we like it or not, we ourselves are tied to the twentieth century. For us there is no escape from the crooners, the factories, the cobalt bombs, and all the other blessings of the civilization which we have built up.

13

DISEMBODIED MINDS

Up to now we have dealt mainly with travel in space and time, and with the various creatures to be found on Venus and Mars—to say nothing of the planets Marduk, Voracia, Plenj, and Thoss. The good old-fashioned B.E.M. was, of course, decidedly solid, and capable of tearing even a toughened space-man apart with its claws, while some of the nastiest of all Martians are those which can change abruptly from one's long-lost grandmother into a blood-sucking scorpion. Let us turn next to stories which introduce mental travel and disembodied spirits in general.

Creatures which live in space are hardly disembodied, but are certainly deplanetarized. One recent example is A. E. van Vogt's ixtl, which spends its time in the interstellar void searching for guul, while in the same book (*The Voyage of the Space Beagle*) we are introduced to a coeurl, searching for id. There is also an anabis, which exists in a formless state and permeates an entire galaxy of stars. It is only one step from this to the Bodiless Intelligence, the mind unhampered by physical existence, and unfortunately the Gloom School has exerted its usual firm hold. Several stories of completely bodiless Martians have appeared, but have lacked conviction. I once wrote one myself, but had the sense to burn it almost immediately after I had written the final paragraph.

Creatures consisting entirely of brain infested most of the pulps, and still appear now and then. Rather more can be said in favour of the group mind, in which a multitude of particles is controlled by a single brain, although the

Disembodied Minds

particles themselves can move about independently. This theme is developed to the full in two of Olaf Stapledon's interplanetary books, *Star Maker* and *Last and First Men*, but since these are in the main 'stories with a message,' they are best discussed in a separate chapter. There have also been accounts of a single, all-embracing Universal Mind of which each of us is a part. This, however, brings us dangerously near the borderlines of conventional religion, and is beyond the scope of the present book.

Closely linked with the bodiless being is the problem of interstellar flight. The relationship may not be obvious at the first glance, but a moment's consideration will show that it is well-nigh impossible to transport a man or a spaceship across the millions of millions of miles that separate our own Solar System from its nearest stellar neighbour, so that unless the writer is prepared to remain comfortably near home he is bound to take drastic steps to free his hero from any physical encumbrance. Supernatural travel is decidedly unfair, and takes us back to Kepler and Duracotus, so that thought-travel is really the only answer.

The absolute isolation of the Solar System is something that we find hard to understand. Planetary journeys are much easier, and we can certainly picture a five-day trip to the Moon or a nine months' voyage to Mars. If and when atomic power is tapped, these times will be reduced still further, partly because of the greater speeds attainable and partly because we will be able to travel by the shortest route instead of in a free-fall orbit. Jupiter and the other giant planets will come within range, while even Pluto, at its distance of 3000 million miles, will not be impossibly distant.

Not so with the stars. Travelling at the highest speed of which we shall ever be capable, a voyage to the nearest star will still take thousands of years. Even if we stretch the possibilities and suppose that we can travel at almost optic velocity, the round trip will still take nine years. Moreover, most of the remaining stars are incomparably more remote, and a journey to Rigel would take 500 years on the terrestrial time-scale. There is also the complication of the Einstein effects.

A star is a sun, and rather too hot to make a landing-spot for the most durable space-craft. Nor is there any guarantee that planetary systems are common in the universe. Recent research indicates that they may be less unusual than was once thought, but so far there is only one certain case of a star which is known to be accompanied by a planet. This is 61 Cygni (so called because it was numbered 61 in Cygnus by Flamsteed, first Astronomer Royal, in his famous catalogue), which has been shown to possess a massive planetary companion with at least sixteen times the mass of Jupiter. The planet cannot be seen directly, since it has no inherent light. However, gravitational pull causes 61 Cygni itself to 'wobble' slightly, and this wobble can be detected over a period of years.

There would be no point in setting out for any one particular star in the hopes of finding a ready-made Earth circling around it. If we went to Alpha Centauri and found no suitable planet, we should either have to come home again or else take pot-luck with another star, involving another journey of several decades. Taken all in all, the idea of interstellar travel in a physical sense is too ridiculous to be taken seriously.

Most Type 1 writers evade the issue by the cowardly expedient of inventing 'overdrives,' which accelerate the rocket to ten or twenty times optic velocity with no more of a jerk than that given by an electric lift. By the mere touch of a lever the intrepid young commander can send the Inter-Galactic Police Ship *Vega* hurtling about the cosmos as easily as a bee can hum from flower to flower. Regrettably, however, we have to admit that overdrives, underdrives, and all similar drives are out of the question, and the honest author has no alternative but to be parochial and keep within the confines of our home system. True, he will soon run out of planets; but that cannot be helped.

Disembodied Minds

One device used now and then is the Space-Ark. This is a spherical ship capable of travelling at a high speed, and large enough to carry a complete colony of men, women, and animals. The journey to 61 Cygni can be covered in a thousand years or so, which means that the travellers must either go into suspended animation or else resign themselves to dying on the way. In the latter case their children will dispose of the bodies and themselves suffer the same fate later on. Eventually, the remote descendants of the original crew will arrive at their new world; but as they will certainly have forgotten the original object of the journey, the whole scheme seems rather pointless. It is rather like an expedition starting under the command of King Alfred and finishing its journey in charge of Sir Winston Churchill. From a social point of view it is, I suppose, possible to write a worth-while story on these lines; but I have yet to come across one.

We are thus reduced to non-physical voyages. I have never been clear as to whether thought can travel instantaneously, insofar as it can be said to travel at all, but the device of closing one's eyes and 'thinking oneself' on to 61 Cygni is hardly to be recommended, particularly in view of the fact that one could hardly expect to find a body waiting expectantly at the other end. Interchange of personalities with an alien being is better, but is more suited to time travel (as in Hamilton's *The Star Kings*), while the space-warp suffers from the same disadvantages as its temporal counterpart.

I have always admired the delightful simplicity of the method adopted by Edgar Rice Burroughs in his *Princess of Mars*. John Carter, hero of the story, merely goes to sleep on Earth and wakes up on the Red Planet, apparently quite undamaged by his abrupt transference across several millions of miles of space. The return is equally sudden, and comes at a most inconvenient moment, since Carter has found a Martian damsel towards whom his intentions are (naturally) strictly honourable. The idea is permissible in a juvenile book, as Burroughs' was, but it is of no use from an adult point of view.

The criticisms I have made in this chapter may seem to be purely destructive, but we must not lose sight of the fact that science fiction is standing at the cross-roads. Either we must keep to science as we know it, or else we must allow our imaginations full rein and abandon the hope of making the scientific story a recognized branch of true literature. The skilful handling of some of the Type 1 themes does not affect the issue.

There have been cases of men and women who genuinely believe that they have the power of travelling effortlessly to other worlds, mentally or physically. Emanuel Swedenborg was probably the first, and is certainly the most famous. He stated that he could speak to angels, and had travelled over not only the Solar System, but also the greater galaxy, learning much of interest in the process. He was taught, for instance, that Saturn is the farthest planet from the Sun, that Moon-Men breathe into the abdomen instead of with lungs, and that Saturnians suffer from excess of light owing to the combined glare of the numerous satellites.[1] This information is hardly in accord with modern research, so that we can only assume that Swedenborg's tutors were undeveloped angels who had left school early. Fontenelle and St Pierre insisted that the Venusians pass the time in making love amid wonderful luxuriant vegetation, while the Mercurians have been affected by the intense heat of the Sun and are therefore fools. An eighteenth-century writer declared that Mercury possessed meat-trees, so that if a space-traveller wanted a meal all he had to do was to spread a tablecloth and let the local birds do the foraging for him.

Travelling of this kind is not entirely dead even now. Some years ago a High Priestess of the Temple of Them, built in London, W.2, gave a newspaper interview in which

---

[1] Actually, all the satellites shining together would give Saturn only about $\frac{1}{16}$ the light of our single Moon.

she stated that she had been to the Moon and found it to be "a radiating station for all vibration . . . the intense silence there is terrifying." And I can cite an experience of my own. In 1954 I gave a lecture to a small suburban society, and spent half an hour proving to my own satisfaction, at least, that intelligent life on the planets is not possible. At the end of my talk the club president rose to his feet and thanked me for my views, adding that I was, of course, quite wrong about Mars and Venus—since he had been there only the previous night, and was on excellent terms with the local populace.

Even now I have not thought out a suitable reply.

14

STORIES WITH A MESSAGE

DURING a broadcast I made from London in the spring of 1955 one important question was put to me: "Do you consider that science fiction is pure escapism? And if so, is it worthy to rank as a branch of serious literature?"

There is more to this than meets the eye, and it would be unwise to make any sweeping generalizations. Some stories are, of course, frankly escapist. Others have a definite message to give, whether or not they succeed in making it intelligible. Books such as C. S. Lewis's *Out of the Silent Planet* cannot be ranked with conventional science-fiction novels, but since they have a basis of interplanetary or time travel, they have many points in common with their fellows.

In general, such works are aimed at the supreme idiocy of *homo sapiens* in choosing leaders who use scientific knowledge for destruction rather than for progress. Even Sir George Chesney's *The Battle of Dorking* (1871), which describes the Anglo-German War of 1875, is an example of this. Chesney tells how the Germans launch a sudden attack on Holland and Denmark, followed by an invasion of Britain, the final result being the reduction of England to a mere province of the German Empire. Chesney was giving a plain warning, and he could not tell that the attacks would be postponed until 1914 and 1939.

In *The Battle of Dorking* the Germans wage warfare in a truly scientific manner, making use of all the knowledge of the period. And at this point it is necessary to say something about the development of military science, since otherwise the 'stories with a message' cannot be properly interpreted.

In mediæval times wars were fought with archery, swords, and clumsy cannon. Hand-to-hand battles were the rule, and, indeed, no other kind of fighting was possible. Each scientific advance was pressed into reluctant service, and even the rocket did not escape, since there is a record of a rocket barrage being used in a battle between the Chinese and the Mongols as long ago as 1232. But though the military casualties mounted with each war, civilians escaped lightly up to the end of the nineteenth century.

The fighting in the Franco-German War of 1870, the conflict which inspired Chesney's *Battle of Dorking*, differed from the fighting between William I and Harold only in the greater efficiency of the weapons employed. By the time the German 'blitzkrieg' of 1914 was launched the entire situation had changed. Before the Armistice destructive devices such as the tank, the long-range gun, and the bomber aircraft had taken their toll, so that civilians were no longer immune. The Zeppelin raids on London may have been mild compared with the havoc caused by Hitler's Luftwaffe, but they were certainly no laughing matter. War was no longer confined to professional soldiers.

This was brought out even more strongly between 1939 and 1945. Apart from poison gas and bacteriological warfare, which were not used simply because neither side could gain much advantage from so doing, every scientific device was converted in order to produce new horror weapons. High-altitude bombers attacked London, Berlin, Leningrad, and Helsinki; artillery reached a new pitch of perfection; the rocket pioneers at Peenemünde developed the V2, and the war with Japan was ended by the atom bombs which fell upon Hiroshima and Nagasaki. The civilian casualties were immense. The Hiroshima bomb alone killed nearly a hundred thousand people.

Whether it was morally justifiable to use the V2 and the atom bomb is still a disputed point. Personally, I prefer Stephen Leacock's slot-machine.

Only ten years after the end of one war we are in obvious

danger of drifting into another. If so, it is useless to expect that it will be fought in a civilized way; anyone who harbours ideas of such a kind is living in a fool's paradise. War is not civilized, and nothing can make it so. Moreover, the leaders of a nation facing defeat have nothing to lose, so that they are unlikely to hesitate before loosing atomic missiles far worse than that which destroyed Hiroshima. The results could easily depopulate the globe, and the picture of a scorched, radioactive world, with a few survivors trying desperately to live on amid the ruins, is not in the least fantastic. It is not the fault of the scientists that their discoveries are misused, although every man and woman must share the responsibility for allowing a few dozens of professional statesmen to risk destroying all that the human race has built up.

Many books have been written on this theme, and the appeal published by a group of the world's leading scientists in 1954 has not yet been forgotten, even though several football internationals and Test matches have been played since then. Science fiction can play a real part in bringing home the danger to the man in the street, and this is the basis of most of the 'stories with a message.'

Unfortunately the Gloom writers again hold pride of place. Nearly always the Third War does occur, and the main plot is concerned with the frantic efforts of the survivors to rebuild. Even Wells's *War in the Air* holds out little hope, since it tells of a world-wide conflagration ending in the collapse of civilization. Nowadays this book reads as little more than a clever, rather unconvincing story; in 1908, only a few years after the Wrights had made their first clumsy hops above the ground, it was definitely science fiction. Wells did not believe that the noble part of human nature would triumph over the evil, and subsequent events have gone some way towards confirming his rather sombre views.

The world of George Orwell's *1984* is even less attractive. Here we have a regimented Police State, with all freedom of

Stories with a Message

thought ruthlessly suppressed, and with science pressed into service by the supreme Dictator. *1984* is a story of the future, and as such it can be regarded as science fiction of a kind. Primarily it is a warning, just as was Wells's *War in the Air*, and—in its day—Chesney's *Battle of Dorking*.

Very different is Olaf Stapledon's *Last and First Men*, the most ambitious of all histories of the future. It is not a warning, but a philosophical message. Stapledon himself was a remarkable man, as I well remember from my conversations with him not long before he died, and as a lecturer he was brilliant; he had the rare gift of being able to captivate even those who disagreed with everything he said.

Last and First Men begins, characteristically, with a foreword by "one of the Last Men," speaking across thousands of millions of years. We learn of the disastrous wars which destroy us, the First Men; of the Dark Ages which follow; of the bland, patient Second Men who emerge at last; and of the various Men who follow, ranging from the part-human, part-constructed Great Brains to the winged, mercurial Seventh Men, who are light-hearted and carefree when in the air, but who suffer the deepest depression when forced to remain on the ground. We learn, too, of the disaster which overtakes the Earth when the Moon falls upon it, and how the luckless Eighth Men migrate to Venus, adapting it to their needs, only to be driven out to far-away Neptune when a wandering body strikes the Sun and causes a blaze of heat that scorches the inner planets to cinders. At last we reach the hour of humanity's greatest achievement, the civilization established upon Neptune by the Eighteenth Men, and are given an inkling as to how the story must end.

All this may sound fantastic, and from a scientific point of view it is. Yet Stapledon's descriptions of the different social schemes are anything but escapism, and all through the book we can see that he is showing us the less desirable elements of our mental make-up. There are weak points here and there, and much of the philosophy will be questioned, but taken as a whole we are left with an impression of power and foresight—much more so than in the sequel, *Last Men in London*.

The theme of migration from Earth is quite a common one, and may at last become a real problem, since we cannot expect the Earth to last for ever. We must remember that we are wholly dependent upon the Sun, and the Sun is growing hotter as it ages. Eventually it will glaze with tremendous brilliance, preparatory to collapsing into a small, dense star with a relatively low output of radiation. For a period the Earth will be too hot to retain atmosphere, even if it survives as a planet.

Some action will therefore have to be taken by any intelligent beings who still inhabit our world. We cannot hope to check the course of the Sun's evolution, and mass migration from Earth is the only answer. At the moment it is, of course, quite pointless to speculate, and in any case the threat is not imminent. According to calculations by Dr E. J. Öpik, the crisis will not be upon us for another thousand million years, so that we need not start to pack our bags yet awhile.

Star Maker, Stapledon's other major interplanetary work, is generally considered to be his best, though personally I would rank it slightly below *Last and First Men*. It is the story of the Universe itself, from its beginnings to its final end when the last galaxy dies and nothing remains. The social structures of alien races, human and non-human, are described with disconcerting realism, although the latter section of the book is so far removed from everyday possibility that part of the impact is lost.

Arthur C. Clarke is another who has described the ultimate fate of the Earth. The scheme and philosophy in his *Childhood's End* are utterly different from Stapledon's, but are almost equally calculated to make the reader think.

Three relevant stories have come from the pen of C. S. Lewis, best known for his books upon religion. Lewis is no believer in actual interplanetary travel, but is ready to use it as a vehicle for a Christian message. In *Out of the Silent*

Planet (1938) we travel to Mars with the philosopher Dr Ransom, and meet with the usual science-fiction characters: evil scientists, benevolent B.E.M.'s (hrossa, sorns, pfifltriggi), bodiless Martians (eldrils), and an equally intangible but all-powerful ruler, Oyarsa. Mars, or Malacandra, is a world of harmony and peace, while Earth, the "Silent Planet" of the title, is possessed of an evil spirit. One cannot help being reminded of how Bishop Godwin's Selenites dumped their depraved offspring in North America.

Out of the Silent Planet is a good story (as well as being a plea for Christianity), but this can hardly be said of the sequel, *Perelandra*,[1] which describes Dr Ransom's journey to Venus. This time the method of propulsion is supernatural. Ranson climbs into a casket and is transported to Venus without any difficulty, while the casket itself is obliging enough to melt away as soon as he arrives. Venus itself proves to be a world in the Garden of Eden state of innocence, and the plot hinges upon Ransom's efforts to save the Lady of Venus from corruption. Considered as Christian propaganda, *Perelandra* is no doubt admirable; as a story it is weak—but to criticize it purely as a work of fiction is quite unfair, and this applies also to the last of the Ransom books, *That Hideous Strength*.

Let us return to the accusation that science fiction is escapist. Cannot the same be said of any novel written without a particular message to give? A book which is enjoyable and wholesome cannot be regarded as without value, and there is plenty of science fiction of this kind.

The rest, the philosophical studies and the warnings, are more important, and drive home the fact that we are standing at the cross-roads. The generally gloomy trend is a reflection of our present state of mind. If we choose rightly, and use science for construction rather than for destruction, we shall find that our ideas of the social structure of A.D. 2100 will change as well.

[1] Recently published in a cheap edition under the revised and more exciting title of *Voyage to Venus*.

15

THE RÔLE OF THE ARTIST

ILLUSTRATED novels seem to have gone out of fashion. Even a frontispiece is now the exception rather than the rule, and probably not more than one per cent. of adult novels have any illustrative material other than dust-jackets.

This trend has at last spread to science fiction, but it took some time to do so. Nowadays so many people have read popular articles in books and papers that the idea of a space-station, for instance, has lost its novelty; yet, as recently as 1945, only the technically minded enthusiast had the slightest idea of what a space-station might look like.[1] The need for illustrations has, in fact, gone. If a scientific novel cannot stand up without being propped up it is not worthy to stand at all.

There are, of course, cases when a frontispiece will be of real help on account of its technical value. Arthur Clarke's *Sands of Mars* contains a reproduction of a map of the Red World drawn by Dr Gérard de Vaucouleurs, and published in my translation of de Vaucouleurs' scientific book. This kind of illustration is naturally very different from a conventional picture showing some particular episode in the story.

However, dust-jackets are of great importance. Here the publisher has the final word, and the author can usually do no more than suggest. This is obviously fair, since the responsibility for selling the book is the publisher's, and his

---

[1] Even now we cannot claim to know much about the final design of an orbital station, but we can at least give a description based upon something more than mere guesswork.

The Rôle of the Artist

firm has to bear the loss in the event of failure. It can neversheless lead to trouble, since it means that a sound and non-tensational book, depending for its effects upon style and true science, may be saddled with a lurid jacket that takes one straight back to the thirties. The jacket catches the eye indeed, but creates an entirely wrong impression.

Not long ago I came across an excellent Type 2 novel. It dealt with the pioneer voyage to Mars, and was technically correct, as well as having an ingenious plot. Yet the jacket was a violent affair in red and green, showing a Mars streaked with railway-like canals, while the streamlined space-ship was totally unlike the ship described in the book itself. It is obvious what had happened. The publishers had told the artist to draw a picture of the rocket approaching Mars, and the artist had done so without taking the trouble to study the text.

While this is an extreme case, it is by no means unique. The position is improving, mainly because artists and publishers have become alive to the danger, but it is still unsafe to judge a book merely by looking at its exterior. The old cliché about a sausage and its overcoat is very true of the science-fiction novel.

Illustrated juveniles are less rare, though they too are decreasing in numbers on account of the added cost. If a coloured frontispiece can be included, it will probably add to the attraction of a book so far as a twelve-year-old boy is concerned; but it is not necessary, and a well-written story can do very adequately without it.

Comics, of course, depend entirely upon their drawings. In general the pictures are crudely done, blotched in lurid reds and blues by artists whose scientific knowledge is nil. The monthly magazines are faced with a different problem. They must retain their sensational covers, as otherwise they would not attract the class of reader for whom they cater, and even if they lean towards the Type 2 story they cannot tone down their jackets—unless they are prepared to risk a complete change-over, which would take a great

L

deal of editorial courage. The result is that a really good story may be found inside a magazine adorned with a picture of a fishbowl-helmeted hero struggling to free himself from the grip of a Voracian octopus.

Technical knowledge is as necessary to the artist as to the writer, and the aim should be to produce dust-jackets which are striking without being lurid. After all, a conventional thriller does not generally have a dust-jacket showing the victim in the act of having his throat cut.

16

COMMENT AND REVIEW

NOT long ago an American friend sent me a copy of a science-fiction magazine which contained a review section. Two books were dealt with, one by Sir Harold Spencer Jones, then Astronomer Royal, and one by a Flying Saucer enthusiast who announced that he had contacted super-beings from another world. Sir Harold was bitterly attacked for stating that Mars and Venus were uninhabitable: "The author's attitude is typical of the dogmatic conventionalist who is unable to see beyond the end of his nose." The Flying Saucerer, on the other hand, was described as "a man of insight and keen perception, who writes so simply and sincerely that it is difficult or impossible not to believe him."

There is no harm in this sort of thing so long as it is confined to the lower literary strata, but it does lay emphasis upon the fact that reviews, like books, must be read with care. It is a mistake to place too much trust in any reviewer. He may be a man who has failed to sell his own books; he may be a kind of King Gama, unable to see good in anything; he may even be a crank.

Serious reviewers of many years ago treated Jules Verne and his followers purely on their merits. In those days it was not regarded as at all discreditable to write a novel with a scientific background, and the general trend of comment was precisely what might have been expected. Then, unfortunately, came the pulps. It was natural for such productions to be ignored, but they managed to drag all science fiction down into a similar gutter so far as the critics were concerned. The very sight of a space-ship was enough to make the serious reviewer wrinkle his nose and turn away in disgust.

Consequently, the only reviews of the immediate post-war period were those to be found in the columns of the monthly periodicals and the fanzines. Only the very occasional book, such as C. S. Lewis's *Out of the Silent Planet*, attracted more general attention. And even after the War papers such as the *Times Literary Supplement* took years to realize that science fiction was no longer concerned solely with death-rays and the Galactic Police Force. The review editors were not to blame, but the situation was unfortunate because even good science-fiction novels were either ignored or else disposed of in a couple of lines.

One particular case may be worth citing. In 1954 there appeared a really good Type 2 science-fiction novel, which became very widely read. When it first appeared, however, the leading critical papers ignored it; instead they devoted whole columns to a book about a minor German poet who died in 1843.

Happily, the present situation is different. The *Times Literary Supplement*, the *Observer*, and other reliable papers have started to treat science fiction on an equal basis with other branches of literature; the wheel is spinning, though reviews are still too infrequent, and the usual practice is to review all the new science-fiction books together in one short article.

On the whole, however, scientific literature is now being given a fair deal, and is not automatically condemned. The stigma of the pulps has not vanished, and a few reviewers are still hostile, presumably because they think that Gladstone would have disapproved of the whole interplanetary idea, but much progress has been made of late.

On the other hand, science fiction is a branch of literature with which critics are still comparatively unfamiliar; and it is never wise to accept any review in a spirit of blind faith. This applies even more strongly to juvenile novels. It is not

Comment and Review

easy for a critic aged sixty to write a proper appreciation of a book intended for a boy of sixteen.

Magazine reviewers are, of course, in a different class. The case cited at the beginning of the present chapter is by no means unique, and in general Type 1 magazines will support Type 1 authors. There are occasional quarrels, such as when a reviewer in the fanzine *Perhaps* described a menace-to-earth novel recently published in London as "peurile and putrid," but such disunity is rare. In any case, I do feel that the reviewer should have looked up the spelling of "puerile."

Probably the soundest science-fiction reviews of to-day are to be found in the morning Press. Here the critic is usually a skilled journalist, without any deep scientific knowledge, but with a good appreciation of what is wholesome and what is likely to prove popular. Besides, he is often too young to remember the pulps, and is thus less likely to be prejudiced.[1]

The reviewer is a force to be reckoned with, but even though he may often be mistaken, he is generally fair. As the standard of science fiction improves, the standard of reviewing is certain to improve with it.

---

[1] It seems only right to add a personal note. So far as I know, I have been the victim of only two really lurid attacks—one in a comic and one in a small library periodical, the *Junior Bookshelf*. Each was (naturally) anonymous, and I would be the last to object. Consequently, it is fair to say that I am writing with an open mind.

17

SOUND, STAGE, AND SCREEN

Until the last quarter-century, science fiction was confined almost entirely to book form. Its very nature makes it unsuited to the stage, and few attempts have been made. The first seems to have been *Wonders of the Sun*, a comic opera produced in 1706, which was an adaptation by Thomas d'Urfey of Godwin's *Man in the Moone*; much more recently there have been productions of the *Message from Mars* type, and it is even possible to class J. B. Priestley's *I Have Been Here Before* as science fiction, inasmuch as it involves time travel of a sort. In 1954 *The Other Side of the Moon*, by Thelma Oates, had a short run at the New Lindsey Theatre, but the main theme was a psychic one.

Sound and screen offer much greater scope. Nowadays there are many people who seldom or never read a newspaper, and rely entirely upon what is prepared for them by the entertainment chiefs. If relatively old-fashioned they turn on the radio and listen to the nine-o'clock news, while if more modern (or if anxious to prove to their neighbours that they too can afford television) they tune their screens at seven, gulping down the last dregs of the after-dinner coffee, and glue their eyes upon anything that the B.B.C. or I.T.A. may offer. If they feel in the mood for something different, they hasten to the cinema and feast their eyes upon a dewy-eyed and much-divorced film star.

Whether or not we regard such developments as being true progress, it is clear that radio, television, and films are with us permanently, and there is no avoiding them unless we retire into a monastery. How do they affect science

Sound, Stage, and Screen 167

fiction? Do the 'tales of space and time' adapt readily to the new mediums?

I am not sure when the first science-fiction play was broadcast. I do, however, remember *The Man from Mars*, a Children's Hour serial of the nineteen-thirties. I remember the friendly giant arriving on Earth, after having crossed from his own planet entirely under his own power and without bothering about trifles such as protective clothing; I remember his leaving again, taking the sinister villain of the story as an unwilling companion; I remember that I revelled in the whole serial, but the twists and turns of the plot have faded from my mind. Then, too, there was Professor Gregory, a soft-voiced rogue played most convincingly by Lyn Joshua; and I have recollections of a third science-fiction play in which an evil scientist first cuts off London's electric supply by means of a ray, and then produces a crop of vast mushrooms which spread like wildfire, causing general alarm and despondency. Plays of this kind were certain to appeal to boys, because they were well written and were exciting without being lurid. Since the War they have died out. Juvenile 'thrillers' with a scientific background are still broadcast now and then, but I doubt whether they measure up to the old standards. It is time for Professor Gregory to return.

Officially, all science fiction in the nineteen-thirties was regarded as juvenile, so that broadcast plays were confined to the Children's Hour. It was not until the eve of war that anything of the sort was attempted in the adult field, but on October 31, 1938, came a strange episode which brought the whole subject very much into the public eye.

It began with a radio adaptation of H. G. Wells's *War of the Worlds*. It was sent out from one of the main American networks, adapted for sound and with the title changed to *The End of the World*. (Why do film and radio producers have a mania for altering plots and titles?) Unfortunately, millions of listeners mistook it for an actual news bulletin, and mass panic resulted. As the wireless continued to blare forth reports of invading Martians, heat-rays, slaughtered humans, and burning cities, things became quite definitely out of control.

I have managed to collect a good many of the American and British newspapers of the following day, November 1, and after almost twenty years they make really remarkable reading. The panic is amusing in retrospect, but it was not in the least funny at the time, since although nobody seems to have been killed there were a good many broken arms and legs, and the damage to property was considerable. At Concrete, Washington, all the town lights went out just as the radio was announcing that "monsters were flocking down on United States soil," and the terrified inhabitants thought that their hour of doom had come. Women fainted, children screamed, and men prepared to take themselves and their families to the mountains, carrying whatever baggage possible. In Harlem, New York's Negro section, hundreds of people spent the night praying in the streets, while others barricaded themselves indoors, blocking their windows with furniture in the vain hope of keeping out the Martian heat-rays.

The situation was not improved by rumour-mongers, of whom there were plenty. One woman in Columbia is reliably reported to have said, "I know it's true. Hundreds are dead. Roosevelt himself announced it over the wireless—I recognized his voice!" Aircraft and robot soldiers were described by people who had actually 'seen' them, and there were even cases of men who had watched their nearest and dearest turn briskly into cinders at the touch of the heat-ray. Guardian angels were also much in evidence.

Some folk who refused to believe in invading Martians were quite ready to believe in invading Germans, and there were reports of Nazi storm-troopers landing in Zeppelins. In one part of New York it was believed that Hitler's blitzkrieg had resulted in the capture of the White House, while at other times the invaders were Russians, Japanese, or

Sound, Stage, and Screen

even French. So far as is known, Britain was regarded as a friendly but futile ally.

We must not exaggerate the extent of the panic. Thousands of folk were too wise to be alarmed, and, in fact, the hysteria was confined to relatively few; but, as always, a noisy minority swamped a passive majority. As soon as the radio authorities realized what was going on, they made frantic announcements over all the available networks, and gradually the chaos subsided. Even so, it was not until dawn the following day that everything was calm once more.

What lessons can we learn from the "invasion from Mars"?

First, the producers cannot be blamed for anything more than an error of judgment. The original announcement made it clear that the programme was fiction, so that most of the panic-stricken listeners were those who had tuned in late. Secondly, we have proof positive that non-existent objects can be 'seen' and 'heard' by people who are emotionally unstable. There is an obvious analogy with the recent and far more widespread Flying Saucer craze. Witnesses have described the Saucers, and even the beings who pilot them, just as Americans in 1938 described the Martian fighting machines and the German Zeppelins. And, thirdly, an actual invasion from another world would find humanity ill-prepared to defend itself, so that it is just as well that any attack from Mars seems somewhat unlikely!

There were inevitable repercussions. Doctors (genuine and quack) reaped a harvest of dollars by selling nerve pills, and hospital surgeries were crowded with people suffering from the after-effects of hysteria. Lawsuits were brought against the radio company, the producers, and even the actors, while the material damage caused in the stampedes took some time to repair. Wells himself was in no way responsible for what had happened. He had not written the broadcast version of his story—that had been done in New York—and he was not even in America at the time.

Although the 'invasion' remains unique in broadcasting

history, and will certainly remain so, there have been two or three related incidents. On April 1, 1940, Station KYW put out a variety show, and the following telegram was read:

> Your worst fears that the world is to end are confirmed by astronomers at the Franklin Institute in Philadelphia. These scientists predict that the world will end at 3 P.M. on Monday, April 1. This is no April Fool's Day statement. Confirmation can be obtained from the Fels Planetarium in this city.

The announcer failed to add that the telegram was part of a publicity 'stunt' in connexion with the opening of a new exhibition, *How the World will End*, at the Franklin Institute. Alarmed listeners flooded newspaper offices with urgent calls seeking confirmation of the report, and matters became serious enough to force Station KYW to make a special announcement explaining what had happened. However, there was no suggestion of mass panic; probably the 1938 scare was still too recent.

Another instance was provided by an American announcer broadcasting over a minor network. Having become somewhat bored, he stated that the Moon was about to fall on the Earth, and that it would be advisable to take cover. The telephone-wires soon became blocked with calls, and shortly afterwards the announcer found himself looking for alternative employment.

Much more recently, the B.B.C.'s famous Goon Show described a Flying Saucer passing over England. The Saucer soon became famous, and many people rang up to say that they had actually seen it. They were soon disillusioned; the Saucer sped lightly on and landed at the North Pole, where the Goons were waiting for it!

The latest attempt at radio science fiction has been *Journey into Space*, by Charles Chilton. Much of the technical background can only be described as dubious, but as light entertainment it has been a great success.

The trouble about broadcast science fiction is that unless

it is to be pure Type 1, it can hardly hold the listener's attention; once the visual spectacle is removed, there is little left. The most dismal failure, to my mind, was the adaptation of Wells's *First Men in the Moon*. In order to help the story along, an entirely new character was introduced to accompany Cavor and Bedford on their journey. Since the plot could be explained only by means of dialogue, there was, in fact, no other way out. The script-writer made a noble attempt, and any deficiencies were certainly not his fault; the cards were stacked too heavily against him.

Since the end of the War 'steam radio' has lost many of its followers to television, and here the scope for science fiction is obviously much greater. A space-ship or a nuclear experiment can be seen as well as heard, and good acting and script-writing can be allied to skilful production. Most famous of the television science plays are, of course, *The Quatermass Experiment* and its sequel, *Quatermass II*.[1]

However, the possibilities have yet to be exploited to the full. No play with an authentic background has so far been produced, at least to my knowledge, and adult television is still stranded in what I have called the Mesozoic era.

For children, the excellent *Lost Planet* stories by Angus MacVicar have been televised with success. Like the books, the serials were interesting and pleasant, and the main criticism must be that the producers were careless in minor details. For instance, the astronauts taking off for the planet Hesikos remain standing upright, whereas no sane traveller would dream of risking the effects of increased g without lying flat. There were other similar slips, and it is hard to see why; all the inaccuracies could have been weeded out without difficulty had the script been checked by an expert, and the story would have gained in plausibility. Of course, it may be argued that technical accuracy is not essential in a juvenile production; but why spread false information when it is so easy to be correct? One

---

[1] Pronounced to rhyme with 'later-mass,' not 'porter-mass.'

cannot blame the author, and the fault lies with the producers, though in all other respects the *Lost Planet* series was first-class.

A science-fiction play is obviously ambitious, particularly when dealing with outer space. Modern techniques should, however, be equal to the strain, and it is a great pity that television has not yet risked putting on an authentic Type 2 serial. We can only hope that this omission will be rectified before long.

Films, of course, go back much further than television, and the first science-fiction productions date from the very early days. Not long ago I was lucky enough to see a film made by George Mélès as long ago as 1904. It was called *Journey across the Impossible*, and I am glad not to have missed it. The space-ship is launched from a ramp in the approved manner, but looks more like a steam-train than anything else, though on one of the planets visited (presumably Mercury, as the voyagers find it necessary to climb into a refrigerator) they are fortunate enough to find a rocket waiting for them, and take off in comfort, assisted by a propeller fastened to the rear of the ship.

However, the first serious production was Fritz Lang's *Frau im Mond*, made in 1929. Oddly enough this film was linked with the old German Society for Space-Travel, the VfR, earliest of the important Interplanetary Societies, and its history is therefore of more than usual interest.

The leading figure in the episode is that of Professor Hermann Oberth, the Rumanian mathematician who is regarded as the 'father of astronautics.' Nowadays Oberth is an internationally famous and respected scientist, but this was hardly the case in 1929. Many people dismissed him as a crank, since he had offended orthodox science by daring to write a technical treatise upon space-travel.

The first scientists to suggest using the rocket to cross from Earth to Moon were Konstantin Ziolkovsky and Hermann Ganswindt, in the closing years of the last century. Neither was taken seriously. Ziolkovsky was a deaf, retiring theorist who remained practically unknown even in his native Russia, while Ganswindt combined so many weird ideas with his few genuine flashes of insight that there was some justification in regarding him as a crank. For instance, he never really grasped the meaning of 'reaction,' and several of his experiments achieved notoriety without inspiring confidence; there was, for example, his helicopter, which might have flown quite well had he only been able to provide it with an engine.

Of very different mould was Robert Hutchings Goddard, the first man to fire a liquid-fuel rocket. Whereas Ziolkovsky was indifferent to publicity and Ganswindt courted it, Goddard had an intense dislike of publishing his results. When he did issue a slim monograph about his high-altitude rocket research, a New York paper came out with the headline "Believes Rocket Can Reach Moon." Goddard was quick to pour cold water on the fires of journalistic enthusiasm, and before long he was left free to continue his work in peaceful obscurity. He fired his first rocket in 1926, but published no report until 1930, and it was not until ten years after the actual launching that his activities became common knowledge.

So far as the man in the street was concerned, inter-planetary flight was still a fantastic dream of the thirtieth century. If it was considered at all, it was on the basis of Verne's space-gun or Wells's anti-gravity shield. All this was altered in 1923, when the Munich publishing firm of R. Oldenbourg issued a thin book called *Die Rakete zu den Planetenräumen* (*The Rocket into Interplanetary Space*), written by Oberth. It was a remarkable volume, and all the more so because it was entirely original. Goddard had published almost nothing, Ganswindt's work was of little real value, and Oberth had never even heard of Ziolkovsky. Yet he dealt with high-altitude rocketry, flights to the Moon, space-stations, and even minor problems such as vacuum suits and conditions of zero gravity. Liquid fuels were discussed, and so were possible transfer orbits. The whole book was completely sound, and its principles are still valid to-day. The mathematical section was equally correct, and despite its technical nature *Die Rakete* became something of a best-seller.

In the sober world of science Oberth wrought a revolution. 'Astronautics' was born, and Interplanetary Societies sprang up like mushrooms. One of the first was the celebrated VfR, founded in 1927 by a group of enthusiasts in Breslau. Oberth was invited to join, and subsequently acted as president.

In those days rocketry was largely an amateur science. Governments and Ministries were not interested; and since the researchers were concerned with the Moon and not with slaughter, there were no national considerations either. On the other hand, running a society costs money, particularly when practical work is to be undertaken. The VfR was in constant financial difficulties, mainly because, in spite of Oberth, people declined to look at it as anything but a type of music-hall.

The pulps did not help. They never spread to Germany as thoroughly as to Britain, but they were influential enough to fog the issue, and it was never easy to persuade the general public to believe in Oberth's rockets rather than in Captain Horror's death-ray. Two popular books appeared, one by Max Valier—who subsequently killed himself during experiments with those singularly futile contraptions, rocket cars—and the other by W. Ley; but these too reached only a limited circle of readers, and the VfR came in for much ridicule.

Consequently, the news that a leading German producer was interested in producing a space-fiction film came as a great relief. Fritz Lang, the producer, had an international reputation, and he believed in doing things on a grand scale. As soon as the script for *Frau im Mond* had been finished Oberth was asked to serve as technical adviser. He accepted, and in the autumn of 1928 he arrived in Berlin, where he remained for over a year.

Sound, Stage, and Screen

Lang wanted some original publicity. The theme of the film was a flight to the Moon; unfortunately, not even Oberth could be expected to build a full-scale space-ship in a matter of a few months, but he might at least produce some sort of rocket which would impress the public and drive them to the cinemas. The idea was received enthusiastically by the VfR, and Oberth, with two assistants named Rudolf Nebel and Alexander Shershevsky, set to work.

It was a good scheme, and had it worked out it would have done much towards selling the space-travel idea to the man in the street. Unfortunately, it did not work out, and nobody was really to blame. Oberth, at least the Oberth of 1929, was above all a theorist; he had had no experience of organizing and very little of practical engineering, and neither of his assistants could fill the gaps. There was also the difficulty of finding a launching site. The first choice was the Griefswalder Oie, a small island off the Baltic coast, but this was vetoed by the authorities, as it was felt that the local lighthouse might be damaged. (It is rather ironical to note that less than ten years later, when the Nazis took over, the main research station—Peenemünde—was set up there.) The Oberth site was transferred to the near-by resort of Horst. The fact that the Oie lighthouse was still within range was fortunately overlooked.

The rocket was to be liquid-fuelled, and was to rise to an altitude of forty miles, which would have been a record for height. However, further difficulties arose. Ley, who has described the episode in his admirable book *Rockets, Missiles, and Space-Travel*, has estimated that even if all had gone well, the rocket could not have been produced in much less than a year and a half. In point of fact, the available time was only four months, and there were several serious setbacks—including two explosions, one of which injured Oberth and put him out of action for some days. When it became clear that the proposed liquid-fuel rocket could not be made in time for the film première, the plans were changed. Instead of a real prototype, the rocket was to become nothing more than a demonstration model. Even this proved to be impossible, and Oberth, still suffering from the after-effects of shock, left Berlin to return to his tranquil home in Transylvania. The film company had to issue a statement that the launching had been postponed indefinitely. Actually, the Oberth Rocket never flew at all.

Despite this fiasco, which did interplanetary research a certain amount of harm, Lang's film was duly completed. It was shown for the first time on October 15, 1929. The scenery was not really convincing, and the plot had numerous weak spots, but from a technical point of view it was a good first attempt. It is of tremendous historical interest, and is well worth seeing even to-day.

Britain had to wait until 1936 for its first interplanetary film, and when it did appear it was a grave disappointment to the technicians. It was H. G. Wells's *The Shape of Things to Come*, and for some reason or other it returned to the antiquated space-gun idea. The British Interplanetary Society, then three years old, was not impressed, and the general feeling was that Wells had let science down badly. One can see both points of view. Wells, interested mainly in social studies, was using the space theme as a vehicle for his own ideas, whereas the technicians were anxious to spread correct information about future events. Since the space-gun had been shown to be unworkable, it did indeed seem a pity to revert to it. Even anti-gravity would have been better.

In fact, *The Shape of Things to Come* was a Type 1 film. If accepted as such, and regarded simply as entertainment with a thought-provoking background, it must be classed as excellent. Technically, however, it was a retreat rather than an advance.

Science fiction did not spread to the American screen much before the War. Fittingly enough in a country still dominated by the pulps, the original films were juveniles, starring Buster Crabbe and Buck Rogers. I have seen only one; there was no true science in it, but it was at least harmless.

Sound, Stage and Screen

Even the three-headed Venusians were considerate and benign.

Post-war enthusiasm for space-travel took some time to reach Hollywood, but in 1950 there appeared the classic *Destination Moon*, produced by George Pal and with designs by Chesley Bonestell. I am not sure whether Mr Pal received an Oscar for it, but he certainly should have done. For once in a way there was no far-fetched plot, no dewy-eyed dumb blonde or space vamp[1] to cumber up the screen, and no glaring technical blunder. It is always easy to criticize, and there were, of course, a few slips here and there, but on the whole accuracy was maintained to a remarkable degree. Even the interior of the lunar crater Harpalus, where the space-ship landed, was shown correctly. Nor was the colour process unduly gaudy.

The story is simple enough. Following a series of rocket experiments, it is decided to send an official expedition to the Moon. A craft is built; the crew blast off; they land on the lunar surface; they make what observations they can, and then blast off once more. There are various twists in the plot, and a good deal of drama when it is found that the rocket has insufficient fuel to break free from the Moon without being drastically reduced in weight, but it is true to say that the human characters are of secondary importance. The vastness of space dominates the whole film. Moreover, there is education as well as entertainment. The principles of astronautics are cleverly explained by the introduction of a Disney cartoon, used by the lecturer to show his big-business backers what is involved, and the interior of the rocket itself is suitably effective.

Considered from any angle, *Destination Moon* was a splendid effort. It was well received, both by technicians and by laymen, and was a box-office success. Astronauts realized that it had done much to spread correct information, and

[1] I should not like it to be thought that I object to sex themes in science-fiction films; but the space vamp has no place in scripts such as that of *Destination Moon*.

M

looked forward to further productions on the same lines, perhaps taking the story one step further—to Mars, say, or Venus.

They were bitterly disappointed. The second Pal-Bonestell film, *When Worlds Collide*, appeared in late 1951, and was immeasurably inferior to the first. This time there were no logical explanations or realistic sequences; we were back to the menace-to-Earth idea, the artificial love interest, and a space-craft designed so as to send any mathematician into a fit of hysterics.

The plot was based on a little-known novel of 1932. It involved the approach of a dead star accompanied by a single planet, "Bronson Beta" in the novel but "Zyra" (!) in the film-script. Having discovered that the Earth must inevitably be destroyed by collision, a group of men build a space-craft in less than eight months and leave their home planet to find "a better 'ole" on Zyra. The shots of destruction on Earth, as the surface is rent by great convulsions and pounded by tidal waves, are well done; but the space-voyage itself is not. The blast-off takes place from a track which reminds one of a scenic railway at a fun-fair, and the journey itself takes only a few minutes, while the landing on Zyra provides a suitable climax. This convenient world is found to have breathable air, with a Californian-type landscape. The final fade-out occurs as the lovers fall rapturously into each other's arms, staring at the glowing sunset.

Then, in 1954, came the greatest film disappointment of all, *The Conquest of Space*. This was again a Pal-Bonestell production, and was advertised as being based on the book of the same name written by Willy Ley. Unfortunately, it contained a large number of major scientific mistakes, which should certainly have been weeded out of the final script.

The story begins with a projected voyage to the Moon, which is changed at the last moment to a trip to Mars. Little modification to the space-ship is considered necessary, and

Sound, Stage, and Screen

the blast-off takes place on schedule. During the journey the adventurers have a brush with a wandering minor planet, which is red-hot despite the fact that it is moving round the Sun at a distance greater than that of the Earth. Mars proves to be a world with a bright blue sky and fleecy clouds; the sand is red, and there are great boulders scattered about. One member of the crew plants a seed which he has thoughtfully brought with him, and in time this produces a plant rather like a dahlia. There is even a violent storm. The crew members themselves are neurotic, and the commander goes mad at a critical moment.

The film was not received with much enthusiasm either by the public or by the critics. It cannot be compared with *Destination Moon*.

Much more entertaining was *The War of the Worlds*. One cannot escape from Wells; he is one of the leading figures of science fiction, and his classic book has become not only a radio play but also a film. The Hollywood production was not concerned with scientific accuracy, and was an attempt to produce the story in a way of which Wells himself would have approved. Apart from transferring the action from England to America, no serious changes were made in the plot, and the result was a 'thriller' which gripped.

It may seem petty to attack *The Conquest of Space* and praise the equally inaccurate *War of the Worlds*, but a moment's reflection will show the reason. Had *The Conquest of Space* been advertised as pure entertainment, I should have had no comment to make. The same can said of the recent *Satellite in the Sky*.

Other science-fiction films of the past five years seem hardly worth discussing. I have seen most of them, and in some cases have even forced myself to remain in my seat until the bitter end. In one film a space-crew is detailed to lasso a meteorite; in another a rocket aiming for Venus lands on Mars instead, owing to a slight mistake on the part of the navigator. A few more noughts added to his calculations would presumably have led to a complete departure from the Solar System, which would have been a distinct relief.

On the credit side, then, we have skilfully made Type 1 films such as *The War of the Worlds*, and, of course, the Type 2 *Destination Moon*. On the debit side there are the screen equivalents of the pulps, as well as films which set out to be authentic, but which are actually misleading.

It is clear that film techniques can play a major rôle in the development of good science fiction, and some of the novels of recent years would prove eminently suited to the screen. We can only hope that Hollywood will take advantage of the opportunities, and will have future scripts checked by some one who knows the difference between an asteroid and an adenoid.

18

THE FUTURE OF SCIENCE FICTION

SCIENCE fiction is international. It originated with a Greek, and was developed by a German, a Briton, and a Frenchman, while in more modern times it has invaded all countries of the Old and New Worlds. Even those who dislike and despise it cannot deny that it is widespread. What, then, of the future?

Let us look first at Type 1 fiction, with its fantastic trend, its B.E.M.'s, and its weird planets. It is still popular, and its followers are nothing if not faithful. They correspond, meet and form 'fan' circles, exchange ideas and magazines, and sometimes attempt to produce an entirely new periodical. Fan circles of this kind are to be found all over Britain, and there are several in London, Manchester, Birmingham, and Glasgow alone. In America the various local circles meet together now and then at Science-Fiction Conventions, such as that held at Philadelphia in the autumn of 1953, and this is also the case in Australia. There have been efforts to unite the fan circles into a single science-fiction club, but so far without success. It seems that the golden age of the fanzines is passing, if, indeed, it has not already passed.

On the Continent there are a few circles in Holland, Belgium, and Denmark, while Sweden boasts of at least ten. Germany and France have their enthusiasts, and there is equal interest in Spain. Even Iceland has fallen under the spell, though it is unlikely that the new interest there was connected with the 1955 Nobel Literature Award!

Such is the state of affairs at the present moment. In view of the tremendous interest, it is a great pity that so much of the fiction produced as scientifically inaccurate and of dubious literary value. If only the magazines and fan productions could be persuaded to keep to technical possibilities, science itself would benefit.

There are, however, problems of even greater importance than faulty information. The main curse of Type 1 fiction is its depressing outlook. The Gloom School has, in fact, established a complete stranglehold, and few stories end in anything but the grisly death of the hero and heroine. In a recent anthology published in London eight of the eleven stories were of this kind. On four occasions the leading character was driven to suicide, twice he was devoured not by bears but by bems, and twice he was marooned on a remote planet without even the comfort of a Desert Island Disk. Yet all but one of the stories in this collection were written by authors whose literary talent and originality could not be mistaken. Why, then, is there this preoccupation with death?

One reason is that the magazine readers expect it. They dislike the idea of the hero escaping unharmed; if there is a happy ending, they tend to mutter "Kid's stuff!" and look round for something more adult. This is probably a passing phase, but it is undesirable.

I do not for one moment suggest that science fiction should be turned into milk-and-water pantomime; I am pleading merely for a little variety. Variety, after all, is the spice of life, and at the moment there is prevailing monotony. One does not expect every conventional novel to end upon a note of gloom, so why should such be the case with science fiction?

Not long ago I had a letter from a seventeen-year-old boy who had made up his mind to become a journalist, and who had written his first book. He sent me the manuscript, and asked for my candid comments. It was not a task which I relished; the manuscript was badly constructed and misspelled, even ungrammatical in places, and the plot was unintelligible. All I could do was to tell him so; had I been non-committal, the boy would have tried to place the manuscript and would have been bitterly disappointed at a series of rejections. I made some suggestions that I thought might be of help, but his reactions were not quite as I had expected. "I suppose you are right," he wrote back. "I never have been much good at English really. Still, I suppose I can always make a living by writing science fiction or something, just like you do."

It was the perfect retort, even though a completely innocent one. It is worth quoting, because it sums up the general belief that in order to write a science-fiction story one has only to invent a planet such as Strorp, Ploop, Plenj, or Thoss, people it with grotesque beings who keep one tentacle clasped firmly round the butt of a ray-gun, and let the plot and style look after themselves until the moment when the hero sinks to his doom in a Venusian bog or is clasped to the red-hot breast of a Jovian firemaiden. This may have been true of the pulps, and is still true of some of the magazines, but it is definitely not valid for proper 1956 science fiction.

Style in science fiction is just as important as in a conventional novel. Moreover, one good idea is not enough. If the theme is overplayed or mishandled the result is a novel which loses all coherence, since the futuristic background is merciless in showing up every defect. Type 2 science fiction is, in fact, extremely difficult to write, and this is one reason for the comparative dearth of Type 2 books. Another reason is that authors of established reputation and proved ability are wary of entering a field which some reviewers still regard as disreputable.

Consequently, a real opening exists for new writers of imagination and skill, and this brings us to the all-important question of markets.

A would-be author who produces a Type 1 story by mixing all the usual ingredients together in a somewhat unsavoury dish stands a fair chance of getting it published in one of the lesser magazines. He can then repeat the performance by mixing the ingredients again and cooking them in a different oven, and he may eventually build up quite a reputation; but it is not a reputation that will benefit him in the long run, and he must face the fact that the popularity of such stories has already started to wane. A Type 2 story may not be so easy to place, but if the standard is high enough, the story will eventually find a home. I feel that the leading magazines print so few Type 2 stories mainly because they cannot find them.

This is no attempt on my part to decry all fantasy. Such a thing would be obviously absurd, but I do think that an aspiring writer should make up his mind just what he means to produce. If he aims for the fantastic, he must make sure that the story is written really well, since otherwise it will sink into the morass of the low-standard magazine and is unlikely to emerge. If, on the other hand, he means to write fiction of Type 2, he must read up his facts from some reliable book (not the science column of a science-fiction magazine!). If he is still unsure of his ground, he should send his manuscript to some competent authority for checking.

Now and again some national newspaper will run a competition for new science-fiction writers. There have been several such competitions during the past few years, and in general the standard has been good. The Gloom School retains something of a hold, but it is a hold which can be broken by any skilful writer who is brave enough to try.

The circles and the Type 1 magazines are concerned mainly with short stories, and long novels with authentic backgrounds offer greater scope for the interplanetary theme. Full-length menace-to-Earth and B.E.M. books are undoubtedly on the decline, since unless superbly done they will attract a limited public and no serious reviewers. It is easy to point to the example of H. G. Wells, but it must be remembered that Wells was a literary master. Above all, it is to be hoped that the ambitious writer will make his story wholesome. If the hero is to be fried by a lethal ray, let him be fried without the accompaniment of gruesome description.

It is often said that science fiction is a passing craze,

The Future of Science Fiction

and that within the next few decades it will vanish completely. There seems little justification for this view, since we are approaching the stage of making our first real leaps beyond the atmosphere. There is an analogy here with aeronautics; flying stories did not end with the invention of the aeroplane.

Just as rocket pioneering was linked with Lang's film, so future fiction must be influenced by scientific developments. We have advanced a long way since the time of Jules Verne. Then, 'astronautics' had not begun, and the aircraft and the space-ship were dreams of the twentieth century. Nowadays the air has been conquered, and we are preparing to step beyond it. The artificial satellites planned for 1957 may be tiny bodies no larger than footballs, but they represent the first real step in Man's invasion of space.

The first flying footballs will carry only instruments, if, indeed, they carry anything at all, but if all goes well there must come a time when it will be possible to set up a manned space-station. Oberth foresaw such a station in 1923, and in recent times Von Braun and others have drawn up detailed plans for its construction, though whether these plans are practicable or not remains to be seen. As research continues, the story-teller is certain to find ample material for new ideas, new angles, and new plots. The science will be there, and all he will have to do is to adapt it.

So far from decreasing, interest in science fiction is therefore certain to grow during future years. Moreover, it can play a real part both in spreading true knowledge and in enriching literature.

The B.E.M.'s are dying, even though they still wave their tentacles in defiance. Magazines will, I believe, turn more and more to authentic stories, and it cannot be long before we see the appearance of the first magazine devoted entirely to Type 2 fiction, good scientific articles, and sound reviews. If 'stories of space and time' develop as they should do, science fiction is certain to regain its rightful place as a wholesome and respected branch of the literary tree.

APPENDIX: A SUGGESTION REGARDING SCIENCE FICTION

On October 19 to 22, 1955, the United Nations Educational, Scientific, and Cultural Organization met in Madrid to hold a conference upon the dissemination of scientific knowledge. I was invited to contribute a paper upon the rôle of science fiction, and this was read in my absence by Werner Buedeler, leader of the German delegation. In the paper I made a tentative suggestion which may perhaps be worthy of a certain amount of consideration. What follows is not the paper itself, but a condensed account of the main points contained in it.

"There has always been a demand for popular books which present the various sciences in a way which makes them easily intelligible to the layman. This is particularly true, perhaps, of astronomy; it is impossible to overlook the beauty of a starlit night, and even those who are in no way scientifically inclined feel that they would like to learn something about the heavens.

"On the other hand, there are many people who find themselves unable to concentrate upon even a simple technical work. This is due sometimes to lack of intelligence, but more often to sheer disinclination to struggle with any facts that are not self-evident. Such an attitude is regrettable, and if it could be overcome, much good would result. In particular, a greater spread of scientific knowledge would lead to the automatic rejection of pseudo-sciences such as astrology, which flourish only because so many people are ignorant of the true facts. It would also force the general public to consider the danger of using scientific developments for military purposes.

"By far the best way to spread information is by the use of science fiction, but it is unfortunately true to say that so far, at least, this has not been done. There are two main classes of science fiction. In Type 1 the 'science' is either absent or erroneous; this embraces all comic strips and most magazines, as well as many books. In Type 2 the background is as accurate as it can be made in the light of present knowledge, and the unpleasant, gloomy trend of Type 1 fiction is not present.

"Not all Type 1 fiction is undesirable. There is no harm in a fantasy provided that it is not advertised as educational. Wells's *War of the Worlds*, for instance, is undeniably of Type 1. On the other hand, comic strips and sensational magazines are not only fantastic, but are usually unwholesome as well, and it is this trend which must be fought with all possible energy.

"Probably the earliest still-read writer of Type 2 fiction is Jules Verne. It is true to say that many of Verne's ideas have been proved wrong, and his space-gun, for instance, is absolutely unworkable, both because of air resistance and because any occupants of the projectile would be killed by the violent acceleration to escape velocity. Yet Verne himself did not know this, and nor could he be expected to. He kept to the facts so far as they were known in his day, and doubtless many of our present Type 2 novels will prove to be equally wide of the mark when we finally conquer space in fact as well as in fancy. A similar argument can be applied to other branches of science fiction.

"Modern developments have made it possible to write about interplanetary voyages without making them absurd. Books such as Arthur C. Clarke's *Prelude to Space* and *The Sands of Mars* have been well received, and as they present an excellent picture of the whole project, they have doubtless done much to spread correct information—more, perhaps, than most purely scientific popular books. But novels of this type are still rare, and are swamped numerically by books of lower standard. The ordinary layman, lacking any technical background, cannot be expected to differentiate between a novel which is scientifically sound and one which is not. It should be possible to draw up a policy which will, however, enable such differentiation to be made.

"To sum up the problem as it faces us to-day: science fiction would well be a means of propagating sound and rational ideas among those who seldom or never read a factual work. Since these readers are in the most urgent need of instruction, the opportunity is obvious. Unfortunately, it has not been used to advantage, owing to the many inaccurate and unpleasant publications which masquerade as true 'science fiction.'

"My proposal, which I make with great diffidence, is to set up a 'selection board' for each country, headed by a chairman appointed by the appropriate Science Writers' Association. This selection board would be invited to pass each published book as 'approved by the Science Writers' Association' of the country concerned. Since only accurate books would in general be approved, the public would be presented with a clear means of determining the standard of books available.

"It must be stressed that this suggestion is entirely my own, and has not been discussed with any member of the British Association of Science Writers, either officially or unofficially. I accept the full responsibility for it.

"I must also stress that I am not recommending any form of compulsory censorship. Censorship in any form is repugnant, and does not enter into the proposal. It would be entirely at the discretion of author and publisher whether or not to submit a particular book. In practice, publishers with high standards would take advantage of the facility, while those of lower-grade books would not; but the submission would naturally be optional. Official approval would doubtless enhance the sales of a science-fiction book or magazine, but lack of official approval would not automatically condemn it, though it would show that the publication concerned should be read with some caution.

"Selection would naturally be elastic, and the best method might be to have two grades:

> A. Books with a thoroughly scientific background, which can be regarded as educational as well as entertaining.
> B. Books which are not technically accurate, but which are nevertheless well-written, wholesome, and of some literary value.

"Juvenile novels would, of course, present additional problems, but these extra difficulties should not be incapable of solution.

"While the advantages of such a scheme are many, the disadvantages would seem to be few. The selection would not, for instance, involve an inordinate amount of work. Authors and publishers of low-standard fiction would not even bother to submit it for approval, which at once disposes of at least 70 per cent. of the books and magazines which have appeared during the last few years. Probably fewer than one hundred books would

A Suggestion regarding Science Fiction

be submitted annually, and with a selection board of a dozen members this would not amount to an impossibly heavy burden.

"There are many factors to be taken into account, and this scheme is merely tentative; doubtless it can be much improved. It does, however, give the layman a way of finding out which novels are to be taken seriously, and it avoids any taint of censorship.

"The problem of low-standard fiction must at all events be faced. Scientific literature has a great future, but so long as it maintains its trend of inaccuracy and gloom its educational potentialities will be unable to develop.".

The proposal was duly put to the delegates assembled at Madrid. It was keenly debated for three hours, and was defeated only by the narrow proportion of 8 to 7. I feel, therefore, that some such scheme may well be adopted within the next few years, unless an improved general standard of published fiction renders it unnecessary.

INDEX

Allingham, C., *Flying Saucer from Mars*, 117, 119
Amazing Stories, 77
Ash, Fenton, *A Son of the Stars*, 10
Asimov, I., *I, Robot*, 138
Astounding Science Fiction, 77
Atlantic Monthly, 94

Bailey, J. O., *Pilgrims through Space and Time*, 94
Bethurum, Truman, *Aboard a Flying Saucer*, 118
Bierce, A., *Moxon's Master*, 137
Boy's Own Paper, 105
Bradbury, Ray, *Fahrenheit 451*, 146
Bradshaw, W., *Goddess of Atvatabar*, 129
Broadcast science fiction, 167–172
Bug-Eyed Monsters, 71–85, 106–107
Burroughs, E. R., *A Princess of Mars*, 151; *Tarzan at the Earth's Core*, 129

Chesney, G., *The Battle of Dorking*, 154, 157
Chilton, C., *Journey into Space*, 170
Chums, 124
Clarke, A. C., *Childhood's End*, 158; *Earthlight*, 101, 146; *Exploration of Space*, 101; *Islands in the Sky*, 105; *Prelude to Space*, 101, 187; *The Sands of Mars*, 101, 160, 187
Comics, 9, 79–85, 161, 162
Conan Doyle, Sir Arthur, *The Maracot Deep*, 126
Connington, J. J., *Nordenholt's Million*, 124

Cros, C., *Moyens de Communication avec les Planètes*, 130
Crosse, C. H. A., *Memorials, Scientific and Literary*, 116
Cyrano de Bergerac, 39–41, 93; *Voyages to the Moon and Sun*, 40–41

De la Fuÿe, M., *Jules Verne*, 47 n.
D'Urfey, T., *Wonders of the Sun*, 166

England, G. A., *The Golden Blight*, 115
Eyraud, A., *Voyage to Venus*, 43, 93

Fan Circles, science-fiction, 181
Fanzines, 90–91
Films, science-fiction, 172–180
Flammarion, C., *Les Mondes Imaginaires et les Mondes Réels*, 43
Fraser, A. R., *The Flying Draper*, 135

Germany, science fiction in, 90
Gloom stories, 87, 91, 135–136, 148, 156, 182–184
Godwin, Bishop, *Man in the Moone*, 10, 21, 31–38, 42
Gould, R., *Oddities*, 117
Greg, P., *Across the Zodiac*, 71, 95, 104
Griffith, G., *Honeymoon in Space*, 100

Hale, E. E., *The Brick Moon*, 94
Hamilton, E., *City at World's End*, 144; *The Star Kings*, 144, 151
Häpna, 90
Harben, W. N., *Land of the Changing Sun*, 129

Index

Holberg, Ludwig, *A Journey to the World Under-Ground*, 128
How the World will End (exhibition), 170

"INVASION FROM MARS," the, 167–169

JEANS, J., *The Universe around Us*, 101
Johns, W. E., 105
Jules Verne Magasinet, 89
Junior Bookshelf, 165 n.

KEPLER, JOHANN, 21–31, 97–98; *De Harmonice Mundi*, 24; *Prodromus Dissertationum Cosmographicarum Seu Mysterium Cosmographicum*, 22; *Somnium*, 10, 25–31, 38, 41

LANG, FRITZ, *Frau im Mond* (film), 172–176
Laszwitz, K., *On Two Planets*, 71, 96–99
Lathom, P., *The Xi Effect*, 123
Laurie, A., *Conquest of the Moon*, 95, 124
Leacock, Stephen, *The Man in Asbestos*, 142–143
Lewis, C. S., *Out of the Silent Planet*, 10, 154, 159, 164; *Perelandra*, 159
Ley, W., *Rockets, Missiles, and Space-Travel*, 175
Locke, R. A., Moon hoax, 108–113
Lowell, Percival, *Mars and its Canals*, 99
Lucian, *Icaromenippus*, 18–19; *True History*, 13, 15–18, 38, 41

MACVICAR, A., *The Lost Planet*, 105, 171–172
Madden, S., *The Reign of George VI, 1900–1925*, 147
Méliès, G., *Journey across the Impossible* (film), 172

Mercier, L., *Memoirs of the Year Two Thousand Five Hundred*, 147
Modern Boy, 104, 124
Moore, Patrick, *Wheel in Space*, 107
Mutants, 133–136

New York Sun, 109–113
Northrup, E. F., *Zero to Eighty*, 59

OATES, THELMA, *The Other Side of the Moon* (play), 166
Oberth, H., 173–176; *The Rocket into Interplanetary Space*, 71, 173–174
Observer, the, 142, 164
Odle, E. V., *The Clockwork Man*, 144
Orwell, G., *1984*, 79, 147, 156–157

PAL, G., and Bonestell, C., *The Conquest of Space* (film), 178–179; *Destination Moon* (film), 177; *When Worlds Collide* (film), 178
Patchett, M. E., *Kidnappers of Space*, 106; *Lost on Venus*, 106
Perhaps (fanzine), 165
Phillips, P., *Unknown Quantity*, 137
Plutarch, *De Facie in Orbe Lunæ*, 14–15
Poe, Edgar Allan, *The Unparalleled Adventure of Hans Pfaall*, 45; *Von Kempelen and his Discovery*, 115
Price, James, *An Account of Some Experiments with Mercury, Silver and Gold*, 113–114
Priestley, J. B., *I Have Been Here Before* (play), 166
Pulp magazines, 77–79

Quatermass Experiment, The (television play), 171
Quatermass II (television play), 171

RAYER, F. C., *Tomorrow Sometimes Comes*, 144
Renard, M., *New Bodies for Old*, 136

Roberts, Murray, *Captain Justice* stories, 104, 124
Robots, 137–138
Romans, R. H., *The Moon Conquerors*, 113

San Francisco Examiner, 113
Satellite in the Sky (film), 179
Science Wonder Quarterly, 113
Science Wonder Stories, 77
Seaborn, A., *Symzonia*, 128
Shelley, Mary, *Frankenstein*, 124; *The Last Man*, 124
Sherriff, R. C., *The Hopkins Manuscript*, 100
Shiel, M., *The Purple Cloud*, 123
Space-Arks, 151
Stapledon, Olaf, *Last and First Men*, 123, 149, 157–158; *Last Men in London*, 158; *Odd John*, 135; *Star Maker*, 10, 149, 158
Strange Tales, 77
Sweden, science fiction in, 89–90
Swedenborg, E., 152
Swift, Dean, *Voyage to Laputa*, 117

TAINE, JOHN (E. T. Bell), *The Iron Star*, 134
Temple, W. F., *Four-sided Triangle*, 117; *Martin Magnus* stories, 105
Thrill Book, The, 77
Time Travel, 139–147
Times Literary Supplement, 164

VAN VOGT, A. E., *The Voyage of the Space Beagle*, 148
Veckans Aventyr, 89

Velikovsky, I., *Worlds in Collision*, 125
Venus Speaks, 132
Verne, Jules, 28, 43–62, 163, 187; *The Clipper of the Clouds*, 61; *Five Weeks in a Balloon*, 46; *From the Earth to the Moon*, 43, 52–55, 93; *Hector Servadac*, 43, 61; *A Journey to the Centre of the Earth*, 47–50, 127; *The Purchase of the Pole*, 61; *Round the Moon*, 43, 55–60; *Round the World in Eighty Days*, 61, 139; *Star of the South*, 115; *Twenty Thousand Leagues under the Sea*, 60
Voltaire, *Micromégas*, 41

WELLS, H. G., 63–70, 184; *The Crystal Egg*, 65; *The Days of the Comet*, 65; *The Diamond Maker*, 115; *The First Men in the Moon*, 63, 66–69, 171; *The Late Mr Elvesham*, 65; *The New Accelerator*, 141; *The Plattner Story and Others*, 64; *The Shape of Things to Come*, 176; *The Star*, 65, 123; *The Star Begotten*, 136; *Tales of Space and Time*, 64; *The Time Machine*, 64, 140–141; *The Truth about Pyecraft*, 65; *Twelve Stories and a Dream*, 64; *The War in the Air*, 156; *The War of the Worlds*, 63, 69–70; (film) 179; *When the Sleeper Wakes*, 142
Wertham, F., *Seduction of the Innocent*, 80
Wheatley, Dennis, *Star of Ill Omen*, 119
Wilkins, John, *The Discovery of a World in the Moone*, 38

Young England, 10